Learning to Think Like a Martial Arts Grand Master

© 2020, EPAKS Publications

Pompano Beach, FL USA

ISBN: 979-8-9897834-1-0

Publisher

EPAKS Publishing

Author

Ken Herman

Illustrations

Ken Herman

Cover Design

Ken Herman

Proof Readers

Alexander Perez

Steven Saviano

Martin Seck

Rob Hartman

Gail Brubaker

Baer Parker

Special thanks to:

those who contributed their time and efforts toward the development of this publication. Your efforts are appreciated and were invaluable to its development. You should be proud.

Also, no EPAKS publication would be complete without a special thank you to Senior Grand Master and founder of the American Kenpo system - Edmund Kealoha Parker Senior: You are greatly missed.

Table of Contents

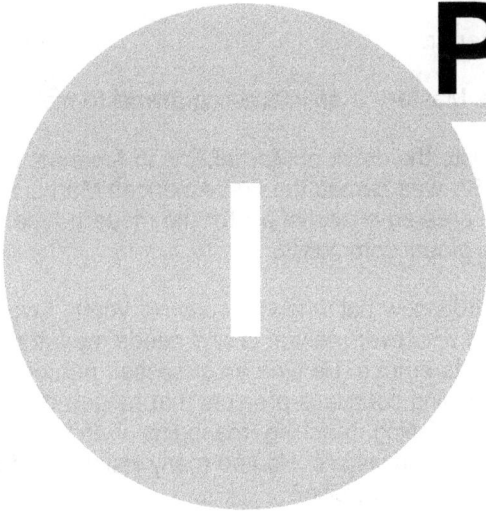

Part

I

Forward

by Ed Parker Jr.

Martial Arts Mastery is an interesting animal to me.

I was born into the dawn of Martial Arts in America. My father Ed Parker Sr. was named the first American Martial Arts Grand Master. He created a martial art for the modern American martial arts global community.

I am in my 60's now but when I was in my youth, I was dedicated to whatever the wants and needs my father had for his martial arts empire. He was an obsessed person regarding his craft. Juggling countless projects that ranged from producing, publishing, teaching, managing, writing or conveying his discoveries and visions. He had many insights and goals that he wished to bring to fruition.

My specific role was to help him document his teachings with artwork, typesetting, publishing, and producing with the skills and talents I was trained in.

He was driven by the desire to be the "organ grinder" and never the dancing monkey tied to the organ. He was a master innovator and never wanted to be a follower.

He was a trail blazer. He absorbed and enveloped all that was useful to him, discarding whatever was not useful. He forged his path to completion in whatever he put his mind to.

Since my father's passing in 1990, I have been witness to his own martial arts offspring fighting over the title he once possessed.

Senior Grand Master.

The country singer Loretta Lynn was often quoted that there are three types of people.

Those that want to be first, those that want to be the best, and those that want to be different.

Unless you are the pioneer of your own path and discoveries; you will fail at being the first, best, or different at anything.

My father mastered being first, best, and different in his field.

The martial arts system that my father developed was named by him; American Kenpo. American Kenpo was an evolution and progression of the Chinese kenpo system that he was taught in his youth.

I was raised in the heart of the American Kenpo community.

Professor William Chow taught my father when he was a youth at the Nuuanu YMCA; in Honolulu, Hawaii in the 1940's. William Chow was under the tutelage of his own master James Mitose when he started his martial arts journey. In spite of the fact that William Chow did not claim the title master, he was a master of his art.

The system of Kenpo can rear its head as an ugly beast sometimes because it's often taken out of context.

Mitose's era was Mitose's era. Chow's era was Chow's era. Parker's era was Parker's era.

Following Parker's era; Kenpo struggled to acknowledge its next era, even though it was right in front of their eyes.

To refine what I'm saying, there were several people in Chow's lineage that created new branches of the arts. We know who those people are. Just as we know who those are that branched off from the Parker system. Which is pretty much everyone after my dad died.

Some of the superstars of those groups can be found in the book The Journey by Tom Bleecker and Joe Hymes.

Others made their mark in different ways. Just to name a few; Tracy Kenpo, Kenpo 2000, Kenpo 5.0, UKF, and SL4 Kenpo.

Kenpo as set in motion from my dad's perspective was an evolutionary art. He often referred to it as "the art of perpetual change."

On one level I love hearing my dad's name in a video, but I don't like hearing the fact that Kenpo is broken. It is no more broken than Mitose or Chow.

The glass is half full or half empty.

Either American Kenpo is half empty, broken, splintered, and doomed, or it is not. To me it is not broken.

I see the yearning in the martial arts community for the next Mitose, Chow or Parker to evolve. Yet their path is to mimic or to repeat what once was.

Sometimes one has to die to surface as that era's most influential teacher (Grand Master).

There are those teachers who create the master and there are those teachers who become the masters and then they evolve to be the Grand Master with their own discoveries.

Both have an important role. Who is to say which is greater? For one cannot be without the other. Yes, we do have influential teachers now that will never be acknowledged as to their true importance in history.

When teachers take upon the greater responsibility to influence the masses and they step out of their own ego for the greater good of all and not just the one, then they can move to the next step by inspiring, influencing, evolving and progressing the arts as a Grand Master.

My dad's point was not just to mimic a grand master in his own system but to become a grand master in his own right, standing on his own innovations, inspiring his own students to evolve as well as he did.

In essence my dad's point was to become bigger than himself.

And he did.

I highly recommend this book and its author as it is an ideal book to read on Martial Arts Mastery.

It leads the reader and student to a detailed road map towards attaining the role, title and responsibility of a Martial Arts Grand Master. If evolving past being the student is your goal, then this is a must read to add to your martial arts library.

I wish you well with your journey to attain Mastery.

Know this; there are no sequels in grand mastery.

Edmund K. Parker Jr

Son of the first American Grand Master

Part

II

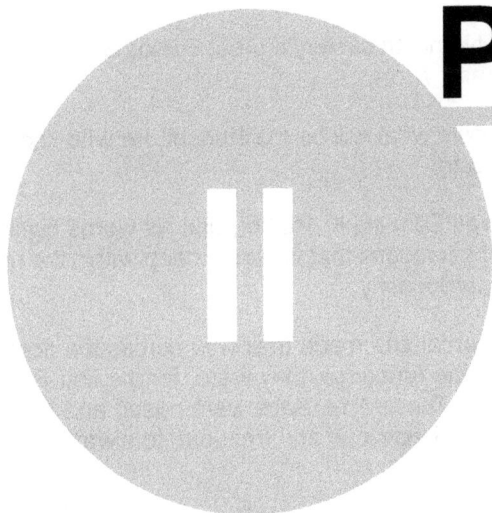

Introduction

One of the twentieth century's great Senior Grand Masters of the martial arts wrote:

"He who knows what will be the student. He who knows why will be the instructor."

That man was Edmund K. Parker, and his words highlight one of the great observations that is buried deep within the nucleus of martial arts philosophy.

When the martial arts made their way across the oceans from the orient to the Americas; they were, for the first time, taught to Americans. These Americans were raised and expected to have a spirit of innovation and freedom; to always question the norm.

That attitude and thought pattern in the martial arts was revolutionary and relatively unique for its time.

Contrast that era with modern society. Now many practitioners are taught to question; and from the earliest stages of their training in the martial arts they anticipate to explore the "why" of what they are learning.

Instinctively most practitioners don't like to mimic the physical information blindly from an instructor, but also to understand the mental information underlying their new art. Most naturally feel that to truly understand the art they have taken the time to learn, they should also explore and master the "why."

Many of the older martial arts beat the mindset of wonder and exploration out of the student. They taught the new practitioner to fall in line and do as they were told - not to explore or question. That the information contained within will be presented in a timely manner and the student is expected to adhere to this structure.

Happily, a large portion of that structure of learning has progressively changed over the years.

Now the majority of modern martial artists, of many **systems**, have progressed toward the "why" and continue to do so throughout their martial art's study.

While this is a laudable and vital pursuit, there is still a large, missing part to Ed Parker's quote that needs to be explored.

What is that missing part?

It might be summed up with the following question:

How was a man of the modern era able to come up with a completely new martial art in the mid-twentieth century that even the masters of the more traditional martial arts had to acknowledge as unique, effective, and innovative?

This book is an unprecedented dive into a mindset that is not unique to any single individual, but still remains tremendously uncommon throughout the world. A mindset that upsets the norms and uncovers some of the most fundamental aspects of how to think and how to understand the elemental building blocks of all martial arts.

Since the boom of the 1970's; the martial arts have become teeming with physically talented individuals, while the mentally talented have remained an extremely rare commodity.

This book is designed to expose the reader to some of the most unexplored and overlooked areas of thought within the martial arts.

A major goal of this book is to help the reader learn to look at common, everyday things from a potentially different vantage point and understanding.

Another goal of this book is that the reader better comprehends how many of these paradigm shifting innovations throughout history were and are achieved. But also, how to use them to transform thoughts about what is currently being done, physically, to the next level, mentally - no matter which marital art system one studies.

But the ultimate goal of this book is to try and enrich the reader's current mindset to approaching that of a true genius and martial arts master.

With all respect to SGM Parker and to sum up the goals of this book, the quote presented at the beginning of this introduction should be amended and read as follows:

"He who knows what will be the student. He who knows why will be the instructor. He who knows how will be the master."

Part

III

Master vs Grand Master

You may have noticed that the title of this book is "Learning to Think Like a Martial Arts *Grand Master*" not "Learning to Think like a Martial Arts *Master*."

This raises the question:

What's the difference?

From the perspective of this book there is a very distinct difference.

A martial arts *master* can be thought of as someone who has risen to the top of their specific martial art *system*.

In other words, they have put in the time and effort to command all the needed information and physical skills to qualify them to claim the title of *master*. But there are no other special qualities or expertise that need to be obtained or acquired to be recognized as such.

Please don't misread the previous statement as being dismissive. Attainment of the title of *master* is a very laudable, prestigious, and a relatively rare accomplishment; and is one that can take a lifetime to obtain.

This is in stark contrast to a martial arts *grand master*.

A martial arts *grand master* is someone who has not only mastered their specific martial art *system*, but has also developed, innovated, and/or stood out within their art.

This is an individual that distinguishes them-self from all the other *masters* for their special contributions, innovations, advancements, and/or revelations. They can be thought of as the *master's master*.

Another way to look at this title is one who has graduated at the top of their class and/or someone who is special among the special.

The title of **grand master** is a recognition that is really not self-proclaimed, but rather one that is agreed to and/or understood by the other **masters** or elite of the art(s).

Sometimes this recognition does not occur until after the individual's passing, sometimes during their life.

Regardless of the circumstances, this title is distinct from, and is in addition to that of a **master**.

> *Note/Opinion: Some martial art* **systems** *have a rank of* **grand master**, *that is not the definition presented in this book. As stated, and as used in this book, the position of* **grand master** *is not a specific rank, it is a recognition of excellence. And, though some people may call them-self a* **grand master**, *again this does not meet the standards set out in the above definition.*

Part

IV

How to Read this Book

Unlike a novel or story, there is no definite sequence to this book. Each chapter is intended to be complete on its own. Therefore, the reader can jump between chapters at will without breaking any designed order.

The chapter arrangement generally flows from more encompassing to less encompassing subjects. Encompassing, not necessarily important! It is up to the reader to determine their own importance to each chapter.

And, although every chapter is thought provoking, there is a *spectrum* of how cerebral they are.

On the brainier side, there are sections that inspire a lot of thought and require a lot more research by the reader. These are sections that can inspire whole new martial arts on their own. They can be thought of as path starters.

On the less brainy side, some sections are more tightly scoped and/or strategy oriented (some might say tricks). These sections often link to other strategies or more broadly scoped subjects.

Wherever there is a perceived cross-reference or overlap of information, there is usually a note indicating that fact. And, there are a lot of notes, comments, and opinions throughout each chapter. This is intentional.

It is hoped that these notes help give the reader a little more context, information, or just something else related to the subject that the reader may want to consider or ponder over.

A lot of this information, although very different, is often inter-related in one way or another. And, some of those relations are not often apparent, unless pointed out.

Also, the subject of the martial arts is huge and this book does not attempt to cover every small detail or potential subject matter.

Instead it's focus is on specific, thought provoking and important topics. These topics might be relatively common across the martial arts; but also, might not be deeply considered, or some topics might even be completely new and unknown to the reader.

Therefore, some of these topics may be exotic, while others may seem obvious. This should be expected.

Regardless of topic, the overall approach is to work toward expanding one's thoughts in ways that normally wouldn't be discussed, written about, or possibly considered by the vast majority of readers.

One final and very important point that the reader should understand is:

While a specific topic discourse may be quite comprehensive at times, it is not intended to be the end-all-and-be-all of discussions.

Rather, the discussions are meant to expose the reader's mind to new viewpoints and/or little explored nooks and crannies of martial arts thought. Each of the discussions concentrates on thought provoking insights, rather than overall completeness and comprehensiveness of the topic.

As the title of the book states, this book is directed toward teaching one how to enhance and elevate their thinking about the martial arts.

From a categorical perspective, this book is far more closely related to a book on philosophy, than a book on teaching a specific martial art or a specific way of doing the martial arts; or even a specific way of thinking about the martial arts.

Note: There is one major element that the reader may notice about this book that needs to be pointed out. This subject is man-made weapons and how they are handled throughout the book.

Where this book does not purposely exclude man-made weapons and their use in the discussions, it also does not go out of its way to deal with and any special nuances that their use may cause on the subject matter.

In other words, this book is not intended as a book on man-made weapons or their influences, but a book on the subject of martial arts in general.

Part

V

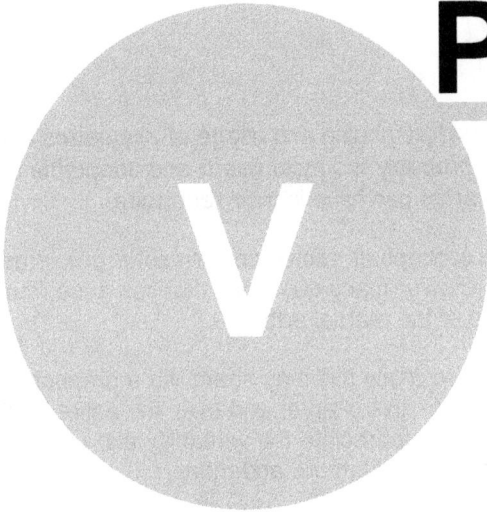

Opposites and Reverses

Overview

A thorough understanding and usage of ***opposites*** *and* ***reverses*** is probably the most useful and adaptable tool that any martial artist can have in their repertoire.

This simple conceptual framework can solve problems, open doors, and answer many questions that can arise from the study and practice of the martial arts.

At first blush, to many this may seem like a preposterous proposal. But, as this chapter and even the entire book unfolds, one will come to appreciate the versatility and ubiquitous nature of this conceptual tool, more and more.

Defining Terms

Before getting into what a useful tool *opposites* and *reverses* are, one must have an understanding of what this conceptual tool actually is. And, probably the best way to accomplish this is through definitions.

Opposite can be defined as:

1. Diametrically different; of a contrary kind or nature.

2. Contrary or radically different in some respect common to both, as in nature, qualities, direction, result, or significance; opposed.

Reverse can be defined as:

1. The opposite, contrary, or complete change of direction, action, or order.

2. Send on the exact opposite course.

The first thing to notice is that *opposite* tends to be a more wide-ranging definition than *reverse*.

The second thing to notice is that *opposite* is used in the definition of *reverse*; but not the other way around.

The third thing to notice is that *reverse* tends to be more physically and sequentially based; where *opposite* tends to be more characteristically based (i.e. mentally), but also includes all the aspects of *reverse*.

So, from all these observations one can conclude that all *reverses* are *opposites* but not all *opposites* are *reverses*.

In other words, the definition of *reverse* is narrower and more specific; while the definition of *opposite* is broader and more inclusive. Or, *opposite* is an umbrella definition to *reverse*.

Opposite

So, how does all this definition stuff of *opposite* and *reverse* help with the martial arts? Let's start simple and then work towards more complex scenarios.

First, imagine that one wishes to create a brand-new martial art from scratch. Where to start?

Probably the first thing to decide would be: would this fantastic new art be just defensive? Or, would it also include some offensive maneuvers? Or, would it only be offensive (i.e. no defensive maneuvers). Or, even to throw a bigger monkey wrench into the mental pot; would it be only a healing art?

Here's where it all gets interesting - how did they come to that decision in the first place? Through the subtle and inherent understanding of *opposites*. Offense and defense (and healing) are *opposites* of one another.

> *Note: Some readers may have noticed that a decision was made without mentioning it.*
>
> *That decision was whether to have an empty-handed martial art or a weapon based one.*
>
> *In order not to complicate things further, that decision was purposely skipped and the assumption is that the martial art is intended to be empty-handed.*
>
> *(And for those really astute; that decision is also about* **opposites***).*

To give some real-world examples of this understanding:

Take Ed Parker Jr.'s creation of the Paxial arts. He came to the conclusion that in order for his new *system* to work within the public school system in the United States, there could NOT be

ANY offensive maneuvers. And, that therefore the **system** could only teach the students to defend themselves with non-aggressive maneuvers.

> *Note: In the example above, even the term Paxial Arts is the* **opposite** *of Martial Arts. As the word Martial is based upon the god Mars, the god of war, were as Paxial is based upon the goddess Pax, the goddess of peace.*

Contrast that with Dr. Maung Gyi. He extensively teaches arts that are solely designed as healing arts - such as Min Zin and Letha Yoga. These arts may be used, in some cases, for fixing physical problems that may arise from the practicing of the martial arts (yet another **opposite**).

OK, we've made a decision, our fantastic new art will contain both offensive and defensive maneuvers.

Next decisions:

Will it include both left and right sided maneuvers? Will it include hands and feet? Will it advance and/or retreat - or stay stationary? Will our hand(s) ever open and close - or, stay open / closed? These may sound like inane decisions and things that would automatically be decided upon. But, no one can debate that they are critical to what your new art will look like. And, they are all decisions upon **opposites** and **reverses**.

Now that we have a basic understanding down, let's get a little more complex, or rather to be more accurate, less obvious; and start to reveal the true power of this mental tool.

Keep in mind that the whole concept of **opposite** and **reverse** is not complex, but rather the understanding of the tool and how to use it is hidden in plain sight to most people.

It's not magic nor mysterious; it's just not apparent, to most, and is therefore often not implemented.

It's almost too easy. So easy, it's not considered or often overlooked by nearly everyone. But, if one gets so comfortable using this tool that it becomes second nature and frequently the first mental tool they put to use, it can change how someone views the martial arts and even their perspective on the world.

To open up the mental door a little more, let's continue with these few scenarios:

What would one do if they are trying to hit someone in the face, but they keep blocking your strikes?

Another way to phrase it, would be:

How does one deal with a situation where the top of the opponent is covered?

Answer: go low; it will probably be open.

In other words, do an *opposite* of what was currently trying to be done.

OK, how about if the right side of the opponent is covered?

Answer: go left, it might be open.

Again, an *opposite*.

Let's continue with these:

if one was trying circular strikes, switch to linear strikes. If one is striking straight ahead to no avail, try downward or upward strikes. Both *opposites*.

If one thinks a punch (i.e. a hard weapon) might hurt the opponent and injury wants to be avoided: open the hand (i.e. a soft weapon) and slap them.

Again, an *opposite*.

And finally, if one doesn't want to fight someone else, but wishes to end an impending conflict: what to do?

Solve it with words or other non-physical means; by either intimidating the opponent or deescalating them, without any physical contact.

Opposite to the rescue again.

More than One Opposite

One thing that some may have subtly pick upon is that when referring to *opposite*, rather than using 'the' *opposite*, 'an' *opposite* is typically stated.

Why?

Let's use an example to explain:

If one were told to get into some sort of training or fighting stance and then to execute a right, straight, thrusting punch: and then immediately told to execute an *opposite* maneuver, what could they do?

> Note: For those readers who are not familiar with the above lingo here is a break down:
>
> * right = a maneuver executed on the right side of the body
> * straight = straight ahead (i.e. about solar plexus height - on a horizontal plane) (within the above example: with the palm of the punch facing downward)
> * thrusting = strike is thrown, but left out (i.e. not retracted back to the starting position - a.k.a. snapped)
> * punch = a closed hand strike which makes contact at the front of the first two knuckles of the striking fist

Most would probably immediately execute the same maneuver, but with the left hand - and that would be a correct response.

But, is that the only correct response?

The answer is an emphatic, NO!

That is only one of many potential responses.

Many?

Yes, many!

To highlight this, let's list some of the other correct responses and delve into why they are all potentially correct.

- a. a right, straight, snapping punch
- b. a right, roundhouse punch
- c. any uppercut punch
- d. any elbow strike
- e. a heel-palm strike
- f. a right, straight, thrusting kick
- g. any block

> Note: These are not all of the potential **opposite** maneuvers. That is left up to the reader to explore on their own.

Let's go over each why 1-by-1:

- a. snapping (retracting) is an **opposite** of thrusting (leaving out)
- b. roundhouse (circular) is an **opposite** of straight (linear)
- c. palm-up is an **opposite** of palm-down + vertical is an **opposite** of horizontal (direction of strike)
- d. strike with the **opposite** end of the initial weapon
- e. open hand is an **opposite** of close hand
- f. strike with the **opposite** end of the body from the initial weapon
- g. block (defense) is an **opposite** of strike (offense)

So, why is this all true?

Because of the definition of **opposite** *"contrary or radically different in some respect common to both."* This definition just states that there must be some sort of common characteristic and then some major difference. And, most things we deal with in the real world, or mental world, have more than one independent characteristic that can be isolated and defined. And, therefore, **opposite** can be applied to any one, or more, of those characteristics; and in any combination we wish.

This is the true power of **opposite** and how to use it. And, with this power comes sophistication and complexity.

Reverse

With all this discussion about *opposite*, what about *reverse*? As stated earlier in this chapter, *reverse* is more specific than *opposite*, but that does not mean it doesn't have some of its own properties that should be explored. But first, let's discuss how it's more specific.

Simplistically, *reverse* can be typically thought of as limited to direction or order and further limited to the exact *opposite*. When applied to direction, *reverse* is the exact *opposite* direction.

For example:

Forward and backward, up and down, or left and right. When applied to a sequence of items, *reverse* refers to the exact *opposite* of the order. For instance, A, B, C has only one *reverse*; C, B, A; and nothing else.

Once this is understood, we can use this to our advantage when applied to the martial arts.

Using the maneuver discussed earlier in this chapter: a right, straight, thrusting punch from a training position. If one were directed to return the punch to its starting position, after executing it - what could they do? Most people would probably *reverse* the path of travel of the punch.

In other words, take the exact *opposite* path of travel back to the start. But that is not the only option. We could take a more circuitous return path. For instance, make a large, circular, arching return path back to the starting point. Less efficient, but still accomplishing the same goal.

Note: In American Kenpo lingo, the two choices would be referred to as:
option #1 - Reverse Motion
option #2 - Return Motion

OK, so what? How does this help? The first option was more efficient. Why wouldn't I just choose that option and forget the rest?

All good questions. But, let's stop to examine the differences.

First, the *reverse* motion is more efficient, but since it is traveling on the same path it took forward, it will probably have a clear, unobstructed path in *reverse* (because it had a clear path being executed). This sounds beneficial. But studying this further...

The return motion may be used to accomplish more offensive and/or defensive maneuvering on its return path - thus compounding the effectiveness of the intent of the maneuver.

Consider, as one possibility, the fact that after the punch, the punching hand could be looped upward, hitting the opponent's chin area, before returning back to the starting point. Bonus points for damage! And in a lot of situations, a better overall result.

But what if one wanted an almost guaranteed, unobstructed return path, because they needed to strike an opponent attempting to grab them from behind as quickly as possible?

Then the quickest and better choice would be to use a backward elbow strike (i.e. the *reverse* motion).

The important part to understand in all of this analysis is that there are subtle differences between the two definitions that, when explored, can lead to many opportunities and possibilities. And, that one should have a clear understanding of those differences and how they can be applied.

A Mental Exercise

In order to get comfortable with using *opposite* and *reverse* as a mental tool, try the following exercise:

For the next few days, weeks, months, or however long it takes for this exercise to become comfortable, natural, and/or second nature; randomly throughout the day, or when it comes to mind, try and pick out any random thing (it can be physical or mental) and try to break it down into its fundamental characteristics and then find as many *opposites* as possible. Try to be extremely diverse with the characteristics: color, texture, direction, size, timing, speed, make-up, impressions, and other individual nuances of the selected item.

After a while, this process should become a habit and a natural step in examining anything.

Ultimately, one will greatly expand their attention to detail and the ability to flip something on its head and look at it from a completely different *(opposite) perspective*.

Spectrum

A very effective tool that one may use when dealing with the subject of **opposites and reverses** is the **spectrum**. Many things in life have an **opposite**, but there are also often many other mental or physical steps between a full **opposite**.

For example:

An open hand is the **opposite** of a closed hand. But is that all? Is there no other positions the hand can be in?

Obviously not.

> *Note: In American Kenpo lingo, this general concept of a* **spectrum** *and/or sliding scale with white, black, and shades of gray in the middle; is referred to as "degrees of x." - where "x" is the subject.*
>
> *From the example above:*
>
> *The spectrum of an open hand would be referred as degrees of opening the hand.*

Because of this fact one should also take the time to find all the related elements on the **spectrum** along with the full **opposite** ends of the **spectrum**.

> Note: There is an overlap with the chapter **Organization, Classification, and Categorization**. It is acknowledged that this section could have been included in that chapter.
>
> But a conscious decision was made to place it within this chapter due to its closer association to the overall subject matter.

Development of this mental habit can be just as important as understanding and implementing the broader concept of **opposites and reverses**.

One very interesting thing about using the **spectrum** as a tool is that, like **opposites**, it can be applied to any characteristic and/or group of characteristics of the item being analyzed.

> Note: One should notice that this tool is also used throughout this book.

Final Thoughts

Without spoiling any of the other chapters, hopefully the reader may begin to see how this chapter sets the scene for, and is directly and indirectly related to many of the other chapters in this book.

Once this is realized, the reader should begin to appreciate just how versatile this mental tool can be.

As progress is made moving forward through the following chapters, think back on this chapter, its exercises and examples, and see if this mental/physical construct can be spotted and correlated back to this chapter. Although each of the other chapters are unique and vital to uncovering the *mind* of the martial arts grand master, one could argue that many are just natural extensions to what is taught in this chapter. And, they would not be entirely wrong.

The problem with the above argument is that it assumes that once exposed to *opposites* and *reverses*, one should be able to extrapolate anything using this mental tool.

Which in real world practice, is absurd.

Sure, it would be nice if all discoveries can be derived from just exposing someone to a fundamental tool: but that is not reality.

If it were true, humans would have already discovered and understand all things in the universe by now; which we obviously haven't. That is why a book like this is necessary. To highlight some discoveries that once exposed become obvious; but are not obvious until exposed.

Also, that's why we call people who discover and explain these "obvious" things; genius, visionary, innovator, grand master, etc.

Part

VI

Perspective

Overview

Succinctly, *perspective* is how we look at things. And as such, *perspective* has the potential to be a very powerful mental tool. It can dramatically change how one views, interprets, and/or reacts to both external and internal stimuli.

If there is one overarching element in the martial arts that one has immediate and direct control over, it is one's *perspective*.

But *perspective* is probably one of the most overlooked elements of the martial arts. And, when discussed, it generally is not from the stand point of exploration of possibilities. But rather, from an internal and first-person mindset. This is like buying a used car by just looking at the tires or the body.

In other words, there is a lot more to think about here than just you. But, in the end, it is all about you.

Definition

So what is the technical definition of *perspective*?

Perspective:

1. A point of view; a way of looking at something.

2. The state of one's ideas.

The first thing to notice about the definition is that it is all about you and your mindset. But more importantly, it is about how you think about things - either in the past, present or in the future.

And, that is the crux of the matter that will be discussed here. We humans have the innate capacity to empathize and identify with others.

In other words, we all have the ability to put ourselves in another's shoes. To imagine what they are going through, experiencing, and/or thinking. And, that ability holds the key to using perspective effectively.

Further Exploration

Your *perspective* on things can change everything. *Perspective* controls how one perceives, interprets, analyzes, prepares, responds, and understands both external and internal input.

In simple terms, *perspective* is essentially the ability to look at things from different points of view. And, the ability to change *perspective* is arguably one of the greatest gifts of our minds. It allows us to expand how we look at the world and transform our understanding from a single point of view to many; with each having a unique vantage point and potential outlook or conclusion on the same situation or thought.

A simple change of *perspective* can solve problems and expand horizons that would otherwise stay closed or unseen.

One very important *perspective* exercise is to look at a self-defensive situation from the actors that are involved in that situation - from each of their points of view. This often elicits the following sentiment:

That's pretty cool, looking at it from both my and my opponent's point of view.

But one would not be completely accurate in their assumption or analysis.

For example:

What if one was watching the situation unfold? Now how may points of view would there be?

Technically, three (3). The attacker, the defender, and the watcher.

> Note: *It is understood that there could be multiple combatants in the above scenario. Two (2) combatants were purposely chosen to make the example easier to explain and understand.*

So, from a **perspective** situation, if we were to fully analyze the situation, we would need to look at it from all three (3) **perspectives**. This raises the following question/sentiment:

Why from all three (3) **perspectives**? I don't see the advantage.

Here's why:

Perspective #1 (a.k.a. first person - or defender): Putting one's self in this person's point of view would most likely be from a defensive and responsive point of view. And literally looking through their eyes, one would only be able to see the structure and movements from the cone of vision from that angle and would be looking for initial moves to respond to and potential counter maneuvers.

Perspective #2 (a.k.a. second person - or attacker): Putting one's self in this person's point of view would most likely be from an offensive and initiator point of view. As such, one would be looking for initial openings or holes in person #1's defense, while trying to attack without creating any holes or openings on your person.

Perspective #3 (a.k.a. third person - or observer): Putting one's self in this person's point of view would allow one to look at the situation dispassionately and find alternatives, mistakes and missed opportunities to both of the actual combatants.

Note: There is potentially another point of view (but technically it is considered part of perspective #3).

In American Kenpo lingo, this concept is known as the traveling eye.

This concept is performed by imagining that one takes their eye(s) and put it (them) on a specific body part of either combatant and look at the same situation from that standpoint.

In other words, move one's sight to a specific body part or point in space in the situation and explore the opportunities from that vantage point.

Tip: The major thing to understand about perspective shifting is that the person in all the potential roles of any setting is you not someone else. One should not stay in a single perspective and image different individuals in the other roles.

In other words, one should analyze any setting from each of the individual participant's perspective as them- self. They should use their person transferred into the other roles - with all their understanding, knowledge, intuitions, insights, and observations.

This technique may seem odd or counter-intuitive, but it is the most effective method of performing perspective shifting.

If one takes the time to think about this type of analysis, it demonstrates how powerful a change of *perspective* can actually be. And, how it can find answers and alternatives that would otherwise probably remain hidden. In this demonstration, staying in a single *perspective* would make it hard to fully and successfully analyze the entire situation.

Some other important things to consider when it comes to *perspective* are; the audience, the location, and the *environment* in general.

For instance:

How would things change if the participants were different?

Such as:

People from different countries, different martial arts, or different sexes or ages.

The same goes for where one physically is. How would things change if the situation were in a crowded bar as opposed to being in a field or on a street? Or even better yet, in an office *environment* or at a wedding.

All of these alterations will cascade into changes in how the situation (and even the attacker) is dealt with.

> *Note: There is an overlap here with chapter on* ***Environment****.*

One thing that should be mentioned at this point:

Don't confuse or conflate *perspective* with attitude.

Attitude is roughly defined as how one approaches a situation - their state of mind. Attitude is emotion based, where *perspective* is point of view based.

One way to look at it, that might add some more clarity:

Perspective can be used to determine the attitude of each participant in a situation.

*Note: Although this is alluded to throughout in the above discussions and definitions, it is worth highlighting that there are generally two (2) types of **perspectives**, physical and mental. Physical being how we look at things from a situational point of view, and mental being how we look at it from a conceptual viewpoint.*

A Mental Exercise

In order to get used to looking at things from other *perspectives*, try this exercise:

For the next few days, weeks, or however long it takes to become very comfortable with this skill; take the time to stop and look at a given situation. It could be anywhere, anytime, about anything.

From that situation, realize that is is being looked at it from the first person and a very specific *perspective*.

Look around and try to put yourself in the shoes of the other participant(s) not only from a physical vantage point, but also a mental one.

And then finally, try to look at the situation from the standpoint of a passive observer.

Really take the time to explore and understand how each of these participants perceives the exact same situation differently.

Getting comfortable with this type of *perspective* shifting will dramatically aid one in their thoughts, understanding, and analysis of the martial arts.

In short, get used to getting out of your own shoes - they are not the only ones.

Part

VII

Environment

Overview

In many situations, there is often one critical element that is frequently overlooked until it is somehow inserted into the fray - *environment*. We often never even think about or consider our *environment*.

Why?

Because we often train in perfect situations.

Flat, open floors; away from the weather; proper lighting; and mostly away from any obstructions or articles that would disrupt our training. And, we even wear the proper attire. Because of this, we don't really need to consider our *environment*. In this case: always in sight, never in mind.

All too often the *environment* is something that is considered as an afterthought; a novelty; something inserted to shake things up a bit.

Just like our modern society, *environment* is taken for granted - a given. But, it shouldn't be.

Definition

Most people have a visceral understanding what the *environment* is, but they can't truly define it comprehensively.

Why?

Because we are never really pressed to have a thorough understanding of what one's *environment* really entails.

Probably the precise definition will be a bit surprising:

Environment:

Everything in, on, or around you.

Sounds simple enough. But take a moment to realize what that definition actually encompasses. Pretty much everything. And, that is what we need to *consider* when dealing with the *environment* - everything.

The above definition often elicits the following sentiment:

I pretty much get the 'on me' and 'around me' part - but, 'in me'?

This aspect of the definition is the least obvious and most overlooked. But, consider this:

Does one perform the same when sick as when well? How about after a large holiday meal followed with a few (too many) adult beverages? Or, with a broken arm, leg, or rib? Given these few examples, It should become apparent that what is in you has as much effect and importance on the situation as the other two (2) components of the definition.

> *Note: There is some overlap here with the chapter on* **Economy, Efficiency, and Effectiveness** *and the section* **Consideration Priority** *in the* **Principles and Rules** *chapter.*

What is on you is probably the next least understood or contemplated part of the definition. This can include your belt, shoes, hat, shirt, pants, keys, comb, and even more traditional martial arts things, such as; knives, sticks, guns, etc. All of these articles could be considered on you.

And finally, around you. This is what most people would commonly think of as their *environment*. Items such as; walls, floors, chairs, doors, and even your opponent(s) are included in this part of the definition. But, don't forget about the more esoteric elements such light, air, and gravity; each of these are also part of your *environment*.

Further Exploration

Certainly, the thing that is stated in the definition, but not really called out is that we are not in a vacuum floating somewhere in space. There is stuff all around our *environment*. And, all of that stuff might be used to our advantage or downfall. But, the most important part of that understanding of the stuff is distance. How far is this stuff from us? And due to its proximity, is it in range?

In other words, can it be used by you or against you? Is it a threat? Or, is it outside our immediate sphere of influence or danger?

As an experiment about *environment*: SGM Parker used to say to his audience:

I bet I can stand within two (2) feet of any of you and you can't hurt me - or even touch me. Does anyone want to take me up on this bet?

Usually, someone would sheepishly take the bet with much nervous laughter from the audience.

At this point, Mr. Parker would put the volunteer just outside of a doorway and then close the door between them.

This would show how a simple change in the *environment* could cause a drastic change in the situation.

Tie that example with handing a person a hand gun, but then telling them they must shoot at you from a mile away. Clearly, the weapon is well outside its effective range and therefore becomes far less of a concern.

These are two (2) obviously extraordinary illustrations of *environment*. And, although the extremes of the examples are purposely excessive, the fundamentals are solid and can be used in far less extreme circumstances.

The primary purpose of both is to open the mind's door into what is possible, if applied properly.

As called out in the section on *alignment* in the *Economy, Efficiency, and Effectiveness* chapter; southern and northern kung-fu are dramatically different in execution. Even down to their stances.

Why is this?

You guessed it - *environment*.

Where northern kung-fu doesn't need to consider a close and crowded *environment*, it therefore can use the surrounding space judiciously and concentrate on long, flowy, and fast maneuvers which use the extra distances to achieve higher velocities.

On the other hand, southern kung-fu is designed to work *effectively* in a very crowded *environment* - concentrating on deriving power in short, explosive bursts.

Two (2) large extremes from a change in the intended *environment*.

> Note: There is an overlap here with the section on *Alignment* in the *Economy, Efficiency, and Effectiveness* chapter.

And one final example:

Why does Tae Kwon Do use the back stance as its major stance? One foot planted firmly on the ground while the other one is used for most maneuvers and strikes.

Stop and think where this positioning would be most *effective*.

One word... mud.

Planting one foot firmly into the mud would prevent slipping and sliding and allow the practitioner to maintain a stable base in a very unstable environmental situation.

Change the *environment* though and the analysis of the benefits changes also.

Final Thoughts

When ranked among all the things to consider in the martial arts, *environment* is at the top of the list.

Its major weakness is that it is so pervasive that it is often never even thought about as a subject on its own. It is often just an afterthought or a what-if scenario.

Ignore the *environment* at your own peril.

It is rarely consistent, although we train as if it is. It is always there, but we often ignore it. It covers far more than what we usually consider. Yet, we treat it like a second-class citizen.

Do yourself a favor, take the time to explore and involve the *environment* in your training. There is a vast array of things to explore when dealing with the *environment* and that is one major reason why most martial arts glaze over it - and sometimes outright ignore it.

On the flip-side, though, when the *environment* is perfect, it can be pushed way down on your *consideration* list. Just don't count on it always being that way.

> Note: There is an overlap with the **Consideration Priority** section of the **Principles and Rules** chapter.

Just a few things that may start one on their way to exploring the *environment*:

Consider restrictive vs non-restrictive situations. For instance:

Can one step back or to the side? Or, are they against a wall, in a corner, a hallway, or sitting in a chair or in a car?

Look at others in the *environment*. For instance:

is one with their significant other, children, or friends? Do those people need protection? Or, can they stand on their own? And even further, is one holding hands or have their arm around a waist or shoulder?

Consider range and how it fits with *effectiveness*. Jamming vs out of range vs putting something between the defender and the opponent(s).

> Note: There is an overlap with **Non-Natural Weapons** and the **Economy of the Environment** sections in the **Economy, Efficiency, and Effectiveness** chapter.

Part

VIII

Rationalization

Overview

This might be a bit shocking (or not), but everyone *rationalizes*. A lot! We do it all the time and about most everything we interact with.

For example:

One may not like their job, but they stay working at their place of employment, even though they are free to leave at any time.

Why?

Rationalization.

They may say to them-self - I've got to pay the bills, somehow. Or, it's really not THAT bad.

Both *rationalizations*.

So, how do *rationalizations* help or hurt us in the martial arts?

It is very probable that every reader has been or experienced this situation:

Someone learns something from an instructor and a little (or big) voice in their head says:

bullshit! Or, (to be kinder) I don't think that would work.

But they learn it and train with it anyway.

Why?

Because they *rationalize* that the person teaching them probably knows more, is better than, and/or has probably got real world experience in what they are teaching. So, it must work/be effective.

All *rationalizations.*

Rationalization can be a big trap in which anyone can fall, either knowingly or unknowingly. Be very careful and mindful of it.

Also, keep in mind what is not being said here:

The total belittling and disregard for everything that came before.

Everything we do and have is based upon the ideas and successful works of others. Be very open to learning from others. Just don't blindly swallow every morsel that is given. Learn to analyze it, understand it, and validate it before accepting it as gospel. And, as part of that analysis one may find that what is being instructed can be taken at face value, or may need to be tweaked.

In other words, learn to question, filter, and absorb information and ideas with minimal *rationalization*.

Note: This includes the ideas and information presented in this book.

Confirmation Bias

What the heck is *confirmation bias*?

Confirmation bias is one's tendency to interpret new information with a bias from and toward their existing beliefs or theories.

In other words, a person pretty much automatically filters and consumes new information with a *prejudice* toward what they already know and believe.

Confirmation bias can be your friend or your enemy: It all depends upon whether one knows it exists and how one uses it - rather than letting it use them.

Filtering new information through what one believes and knows can be very good. It helps one discard or interpret new stuff so that it bolsters their store of information and firms up their beliefs.

But, always be aware that it may also prevent them from looking at that information from a different viewpoint - hastily rejecting it, misinterpreting it, or misunderstanding it.

And, that can be unfortunate.

Why?

Because that new information may have been something, that if looked at from an altered angle and/or mindset, could have helped, answered a question, and/or solved a problem they didn't even know they had.

In other words, don't keep an open mind; keep a mind that is constantly self aware of its biases, and open to challenges.

> *Note: There is a potential overlap here with the chapter on **Perspective**.*

Exercise:

Occasionally remind yourself as to what is being said here; especially when confronted with new information. Always remember that one doesn't have to change their beliefs and include others; just that they need to be aware of their biases and use them to their advantage.

In Short, always try to be mindful of biases. Don't fool yourself into thinking one is being open (including yourself), when they are not. Be fully aware of decisions and why they are made.

> *Opinion: Knowing about and understanding **confirmation bias** will help one not only in the martial arts, but also in their daily life. Identifying **confirmation bias** in not only one's self, but in others is a good habit to develop. It's a handy skill to have and can be used in a wide variety of ways.*

To look at it from a slightly different angle:

Confirmation bias is a form of *rationalization*. We *rationalize* the discounting of opposing thoughts by not taking the time to fully vet this information before rejecting it. And like *rationalization*, *confirmation bias* is everywhere and with everyone, covering almost any subject or idea.

Learn to quickly recognize *confirmation bias*, both in yourself and in others.

Prejudice

Prejudices are something we all develop over the course of our lives. We all create opinions about things: some of which we have never directly experienced or even given much thought to or about. We may have developed specific *prejudices* through second hand information, from a trusted individual, or a single interaction. Either way, *prejudices* influence our actions and thoughts about specific things.

Prejudice is really just another form of *rationalization*. And like *rationalization*, we must be keenly aware of its presence in our dealings in the martial arts.

How many readers don't like a particular martial art *system*? Why isn't it liked?

They may never have trained in it, but somehow, they developed a dislike for it. And the opposite is also true - one may like a particular martial art *system*, even though they know very little about it.

Both are a form of *prejudice*. And, just like *rationalization* and *confirmation bias*, one should always be aware of what and how *prejudice* influences your decisions, thoughts, and actions.

It is almost impossible to not develop *prejudices*.

And, what is being said is not that we shouldn't develop them, just like *rationalization* and *confirmation bias*, we should be self-aware of these influences. We should learn to control them and not let them control us.

We should be aware of discounting, ignoring, or accepting of information, based upon preconceived biases that we are not in control of (or often aware of).

Final Thoughts

If one stops to think about the general theme of this chapter, it is:

Learning to understand and control the *mind* is just as important as learning to understand and control the physical body.

Our *minds* are amazing and complex mechanisms, but we all too often make decisions about things that we are not entirely aware of, or are in control of, often because we have put our *minds* into "auto-pilot".

Being cognizant of this fact and learning to be more conscious of our *rationalizations*, biases, and *prejudices* is a good first step into making thoughtful decisions about our acquiring of new information and our understanding of our arts.

Exercise: Just like the exercise presented in the section on *confirmation bias*:

When learning new things or when presented with new information or situations, stop and take a moment to acknowledge how you think and feel about this; and more importantly, why. Take some time to try and uncover the root cause(s) as to what major factors influence your feelings and decisions about this information or situation.

Also, take the time to try and understand the origin of these major factors.

Opinion: *What one uncovers in the above exercise, the root reasoning, may be surprising. But, understanding why one thinks and feels a specific way will move one closer to being in full control and completely self-aware. Learning to be in control of our bodies is not even half the battle. Being in full control of our **minds** is a far more difficult goal to achieve.*

*But, seeing as our **minds** control our bodies, it is definitely a worth-while goal to seek.*

Part

IX

Economy, Efficiency, and Effectiveness

Overview

The general theme of this chapter can be summed up with the following simple and often used phrase:

Be the best that you can.

Sounds simple and innocuous, until one dives into the details, that is.

How does one accomplish this?

There are literally tons of self-help books trying to answer that simple question - how? And each one has their own, unique take on the answer. Its up to the reader to determine which, if any, fits their needs "to be your best."

Fortunately, our focus will not fall into those books' strategy of "being your best." Rather, this chapter will focus on training your *mind* to recognize inefficiency, waste, and ineffectiveness; primarily in action, but also in thought. But, just like the self-help books there are many opinions in achieving the lofty goal of "being your best", and just many roads one can take to attain it.

This chapter, in contrast, will not attempt to give the reader a road nor opinion, just the recognition of reality and facts. It is up to the reader to use this knowledge on their journey down their own path.

With all that, the main thing one should keep in mind about this chapter is that it is primarily focused on the recognition and elimination of waste and enhancing action.

Another way to look at it is:

Recognizing and enhancing the effective, while minimizing and/or eliminating the ineffective.

But the reader should always remember that elimination of waste and enhancing *effectiveness* is a means to an end, and therefore the *opposite* can also be a means to a different end.

For instance, a practitioner may purposely employ relatively wasteful and ineffective maneuvers to confound, distract, and/or take advantage. This chapter recognizes this action as a potential *strategy*, but does not explore this strategy any further. Instead, it examines the recognition, elimination, and enhancement of actions outside of this specialized tactic.

> Note: Although a majority of the following discussions in this chapter refer to offensive action; the same analysis can also be effectively applied to defensive action - and vice-versa.

Defining Terms

Before diving into the details, one must first understand the framework and boundaries from which this chapter is structured. And therefore, it is essential to define the main terms used throughout this chapter.

Economy can be defined as:

1. The careful and practical management of available resources or assets.

Efficiency can be defined as:

1. Able to accomplish something with the least waste of time and effort; competency in performance.

Effectiveness can be defined as:

1. The degree to which something is successful in producing a desired result; success.

In other words, and for our purposes:

Economy is doing stuff without waste.

Efficiency is getting rid of waste in stuff

Effectiveness is doing stuff more successfully.

The first two definitions are pretty close to one another and might, in certain circumstances, be used interchangeably. From a simplistic point of view, they are just about not being wasteful.

On the other hand, the third definition is about being more successful, or getting a better result. Just like almost everything in this chapter - sounds easy. But, just like enacting the simple phrase mentioned at the beginning of this chapter, the catch is in the details.

Economy

In this section, *economy* will primarily concentrate on the elimination of unnecessary power when performing actions and maneuvers; specifically, in the context of the martial arts. Although *economy* can, and is often, specifically used for motion (a.k.a. economy of motion), this chapter will delegate that responsibility to the section on *efficiency*.

In other words, for the purposes of this chapter; *economy* = "reduction of energy usage" as an applied rule.

One argument that might be leveled about *economy* is:

There are hard *systems*, soft *systems*, and medium *systems*; wouldn't anything but a soft *system* be wasting energy and break the concept of *economy*?

The simple answer is, no.

The more complex answer is that each *system* has determined what level of energy that is needed in order to make the *system* effective. One simply needs to fully understand the objectives and *strategies* of each *system* prior to making any assessment about the application of *economy*. Defying *economy* would most likely come into play by an individual practitioner using more energy than was necessary to make any maneuver(s) effective for the *system*.

Further Exploration

Although *economy* sounds like a simple concept, like all seemingly simple topics, there is always more and more complexity as one explores the subject further. As usual, the best place to start is to give the parameters in which this concept will be investigated.

For our purposes, we will look at *economy* from three angles: *economy* of yourself, *economy* of others, and use of your environment.

> *Note: Some readers may have noticed that the last sentence uses a variation of the tool presented in the chapter on* **perspective**. *This use is purposeful and illustrative. It is intended to show that like many things in life, useful things and tools can be used in wide variety and seemingly unrelated situations. In other words, it is intended to help one recognize and appreciate that there are many other situations where the diverse set of tools presented in this book can be used outside of the simple examples provided in the chapter on that subject.*

Economy of Yourself

Economy of yourself is absolutely the "biggest bang for your buck" consideration in the subject of *economy*. That is because it is the one element that is completely under your control: where other considerations may be only partially or not at all under your sphere of influence; depending upon circumstances.

As a matter of fact, one of the primary principles of all the martial arts is control of yourself (a.k.a. self-control). But again, the catch is in the details. And that fact is a major reason we have so many different *systems* and *styles* of martial arts.

Learning to control yourself is one of the major reasons there are martial arts. And, as most readers are probably already aware - in order to control others, one must first learn to control them-self. And, not just physically, but mentally.

Non-Physical

First, let's look at mental *economy of yourself* in relation to a conflict. Is one relaxed? Is their brain running 100mph? Or, are they cool and collected? Are they intimidated? Or, are they looking forward to the confrontation? Have they had an alcoholic beverage recently? Or, taken any drugs? What is their heart rate?

All of these, and more, dramatically effect one's mentally - and therefore will alter how they will act physically.

As a martial artist, we tend to ignore, downplay, or compensate for the self-mental factor when it comes to self-defense. Our mental state dramatically effects our physical state. The internal chemical and physical effects from the state of our minds are dramatic. Some common, but unspoken, reactions to mental stress due to conflict are: tunnel vision, loss of fine motor skills, self-defecation and urination, just to name a few.

> *Note: A very good book that spends a lot of time and detail about mental aspects of warriors and the physical consequences is "On Combat" by Lt. Col. Dave Grossman. He has a second book that is also highly recommended reading - "On Killing."*

Learning to understand the mental aspect of conflict and how it affects what we do and how we react is vital to any martial art.

To quote Mike Tyson:

"Everyone has a plan until they get punched in the mouth."

It cannot be understated that mental factors prior to and during a conflict can be the difference between life and death; success and failure. And *strategies* to help in this matter are critical.

Needless to say, this is a large, detailed, and nuanced subject. And, like many aspects of this book, would take an entire book in and of itself to give it any justice. Because of this, the subject's coverage in this chapter is intentionally superficial and only the first stepping stone into recognizing and starting the reader on the road to thinking about *non-physical* issues and their effect on *economy*, and combat in general, in a practical and honest manner.

Physical

From the first-person *perspective* (a.k.a. your point of view), physical *economy* can be enhanced by the efforts one makes to remove wasted power and/or enhance the power they will already expend in execution of their martial art.

Another way to think about this is:

Either find where you are wasting power and/or look at ways to change what is being done to make it more *effective* with the same (or less) output of power.

Again, sounds simple, but how does one go about achieving this?

The removal of wasted power can be achieved by first analyzing action, recognizing where power output can be adjusted, followed by taking measures to modify the required power to accomplish the intended goal.

In other words, learn to understand how to regulate power output *effectively*.

Sounds great, one might say - but when do I do this? In the middle of a fight? I don't think so.

Total agreement.

At first, one should do this analysis during training periods, when time and success are not critical factors. This allows the practitioner the ability to learn to recognize waste and work out ways to eliminate it; without the worry of the analysis getting in the way. But, ultimately, it should be the goal of the practitioner to recognize and eliminate waste "on the fly" or relatively *spontaneously*.

Attaining this goal is done through practice and repetition to the point where recognition and correction becomes second nature and more like a natural *reflex*.

Another way to achieve a similar goal, but through different means, is to analyze action being taken and then consider modifications / alterations to the action that may make the action more *effective*.

A few of the things to reflect upon in action are: hardness of target to hardness of weapon, amount of surface contact of weapon, distance of travel, speed of travel, alignment of weapon, angle of contact, and *timing* of action.

> *Note: The above two paragraphs have some major intersection with the chapter on **spontaneity**. This is through the understanding of regulation and modification - a.k.a. **formulation**. The use of these tools could be called **spontaneous effectiveness** and **efficiency**.*

Let's take a little bit to reflect upon some of these elements of action. Hopefully, this will open some doors of thought for your own contemplation on this subject.

Please keep that in mind, these musings are not intended to be exhaustive. But rather, help the reader with places to start their own reflections and investigations into the subject.

Another thing to consider about this overview is that each of these elements may be considered independently, or in tandem with the other elements, and in any combination.

In other words, there is a lot to investigate here.

> *Note: The following paragraphs have a potential large overlap with the chapter on **Fundamentals**.*

First, hardness of target to hardness of weapon.

When striking an opponent, there are three primary types of targets: muscular, skeletal, and organ (e.g. neurovascular system, spleen, kidneys, skin, eyes, etc.). Each target type has specific characteristics that can be exploited in different ways.

For instance, skeletal is the hardest and most likely requires a harder weapon in order to injure and/or break. Whereas, muscular and organ targets are softer and could be hurt using softer weapons. But organ targets, specifically neurovascular, typically require more precise strikes; whereas skeletal and muscular strikes can typically be less precise.

But let's flip these thoughts on their head (*opposite* again):

Probably the most important consideration is - your weapons have the potential to be injured / damaged, also. For instance, hitting a hard target, like the skull, with a slightly softer target, like a knuckle, could break the knuckle and not the skull. Obviously, this is not the scenario intended; but situations like this should be considered.

Next, amount of surface contact of weapon. Smaller surface area weapons can generate more penetration and more precision and should require less energy to execute, but are typically more prone to injury, themselves. But larger surface area weapons may not have the same penetration and would require more energy to be executed *effectively*, but could, by definition, injure a larger area on the opponent.

Next, distance and speed. These are often inter-related. More distance typically allows for more speed, but also takes more *time* (and potentially more energy). Less distance is quicker (and potentially less energy), but requires more skill to execute *effectively*.

Skill, you may say? "How?

Ever hear of the one-inch punch? Not everyone can pull this punch off. But, some skilled practitioners can. There are many, many characteristics to *effectively* executing it. But, two elements that are very important to our current discussion - muscle tightness and muscle resistance.

Learning to relax the muscles that hinder the execution (until needed), while simultaneously enacting the muscles that are required to execute the action (until no longer needed) is a skill that is overlooked by many, but changes everything about weapon execution.

> *Note: There is an overlap with the section on **Distance and Time** in the **Efficiency** section of this chapter.*

Some advanced practitioners learn to engage the "twitcher" muscles in order to bring their weapons to full speed in less *distance and time*, while expending less energy to do so.

This is a skill, like any other, and requires training and practice to perfect. It is left up to the reader to research this skill further. Just let it be said that this is a very *effective*, *efficient*, and powerful skill to put into your toolbox.

Next, *alignment* of weapon. This will be covered more extensively in the *effectiveness* section of this chapter, but the one thing that should be stated here is that proper *alignments* can be a major factor in the amount of energy one needs to execute many weapons.

Allowing the mass of your body (or gravity) to aid in "backing-up" a weapon can make a world of difference in effect on the opponent and the amount of energy required to make a weapon *effective*.

And finally, like the previous point, *environment* will be covered more extensively elsewhere, but *environment* is one of the key elements to consider in all of this, because it has a major effect upon everything one does. One should learn to use the *environment* to their advantage, whenever possible.

> *Note: There is a potential large overlap with the section on **Timing** in the **Effectiveness** section of this chapter.*

Preventative and Anticipatory Moves

Another thing to consider with *economy of self* is dissuasion or deterrence. This is the act of trying to prevent or manipulate action before it occurs. This subject analysis generally falls into one of two types: *anticipatory* or *preventative* - and can be physical or non-physical.

The non-physical type will be covered in the *Economy of Others / Non-physical* section of this chapter.

Preventative physical motion (a.k.a. checking) can be defined as preventing or hindering in some way the physical motion of your opponent. This can be done with anything in your *environment*, but most typically with a part of your body; and typically involves contact with the opponent. Plus, as the definition states, it is done to incumber your opponent's physical movement in some way. From an *economy perspective*, sometimes it is much easier to prevent something from happening, rather than react to it after the fact. In other words, sometimes it can be much more *economical* to just stop expected motion, than to try and deflect or defend against it. An example of *preventative* physical motion: placing your hand against your opponent's arm and pressing (with whatever pressure one feels is necessary to succeed) the arm against the opponent's body.

Anticipatory physical motion (a.k.a. cover) can be defined as the purposeful placement of anything for the intention of getting in the way of the opponent's movement. Again, this can be done with anything in your *environment*, but most typically with a part of your body. Unlike a *preventative* physical motion, *anticipatory* physical motion does not need physical contact. An example of *anticipatory* physical motion: dropping your arm over your ribs to prevent an anticipated punch from hitting the perceived target(s).

So, the question arises: What's the big difference? The quick answer: They are pretty much the same. Yes, to be fair, the difference between the two types is subtle, but have a very different effect upon *economy* and *strategy*. One tries to actively stop future motion, while the other just intentionally gets in the way of future motion. In certain situations, a very distinct and important difference - and technically, *opposites* of each other.

> *Note: One major consideration between the two maneuvers is that anticipatory motion will most likely cause a change of target, where preventative will most likely force a change of weapon.*

> *Note: The reader should also consider this section's discussion in concert with the discussion of **Non-natural weapons** and **Economy of the Environment**. Also, keep in mind that in this context multiple opponents would fall into **economy of the environment**. For example: One can use an opponent as a shield against another, or make an opponent strike another.*

> *Note: The reader should also consider the **opposite** strategy to these maneuvers - **baiting**. For more information on **baiting**, see the **baiting** discussion in the **Effectiveness** section of this chapter.*

Non-Natural Weapons

One major consideration about *economy of self* is the use of *non-natural weapons*. These are basically just what they sound like: weapons that are not part of our physical body. Things that fall into this category are: knives, guns, sticks, pens, keys, belts, shoes, combs, etc. So, how does this fit with *economy of yourself*? Answering these following questions will help in understanding: "Does a stick extend one's reach?" "Does one have to hit as hard with a knife as with their hand?" "Does a kick with shoes on hurt more than with bare feet?"

The general answer behind each of these questions exposes the fact that *non-natural weapons* can, from one *perspective*, super-charge our natural weapons, if used properly. That is why there are so many weapons based martial arts. But that does not mean that one has to create a martial art around *non-natural weapons*. Just that learning to take advantage of a readily available item can allow one to expend less energy and be just as, if not more, *effective* - and simultaneously be more *economical*.

> Note: One large element that is purposely excluded from this section, but will be included in the section on *environment*, is using your surroundings as a weapon.

As an exercise: right now, look at yourself and your immediate surroundings. Figure out what can be used instantly as a weapon. If one does this exercise correctly, they should probably come to the conclusion that almost anything can be used for this purpose. Therefore, one should logically conclude that the skill is not really learning how to use a specific weapon well, but rather, how to most successfully spot and use just about anything to one's advantage; as quickly as possible.

*Note/Opinion: One major down-side to using **non-natural weapons** is the forgetting of natural weapons during the use of a **non-natural weapon**. In other words, just because one has a knife in their hand, doesn't mean all the other, natural weapons are useless. Use them too.*

Economy of Others

One thing that was purposely overlooked until now is - not only should one be able to recognize and eliminate waste in themself; they should also be able to recognize waste in their students; and more importantly, in their opponent(s). And with regards to one's opponent (and maybe their students), one should seize upon waste and use it to yourself be more *economical*, *efficient*, and *effective*.

The above discourse can often elicit the following sentiment:

OK, I can see how I could recognize waste in another, and I can see how I can make my students more *economical*, if I wanted to: but an opponent? I don't really see it being that big of a deal. And, I'm definitely not going to help them be more *economical* in their movements.

And one would be right in this sentiment. But, one very important part of recognizing imperfections in an opponent is not how one can help them, but rather, how can they be exploited. And, these flaws can come in many forms - both mental and physical.

> *Note: Some readers may have caught that the section on* ***Economy of Yourself*** *did not discuss mental economy of yourself. That was purposely omitted until this point. It is left up to the reader to apply the same techniques presented here on effecting your opponent to yourself.*
>
> *Always remember - What you can do to your opponent, your opponent can do to you.*

Non-Physical

First, let's assess the mental *economy* in a fictional opponent. Is your opponent focused or distracted? Do they seem hesitant or resistant to physical action? Do they seem to be level headed or anxious? Are they sober or not? Can they be manipulated verbally? For instance, can they be intimidated, dissuaded, or delayed from action.

Understanding the mental state of your opponent and finding ways to exploit their current condition is an area many martial arts avoid, miss, or not take into account. Most assume a normal, sober, focused, unwavering, level-headed opponent. But in the real world, this is very rarely the case. And, therefore there should be provisions and *strategies* for exploitation of these alternate states. Even the slightest distraction or mental delay of your opponent could mean the difference between success and failure.

And, anything in the *environment* could be used to aid in that disruption - including you.

> Note: One major thing that is not discussed at this point, but should be considered is *timing*. The state of your opponent may drastically alter your opponent's ability to perform and react and therefore potentially alter the *timing* of your actions; be they physical or verbal - offensive, defensive, and/or reactionary.

Sometimes the most *economical* action is verbal, not physical. The vast majority of martial arts only have physical training, but almost totally ignore the verbal aspects of self-defense. Many physical confrontations could be dissuaded from even occurring, or an outcome altered, if the martial arts practitioner only spent more time learning how to control an opponent verbally and with other non-confrontational (or confrontational) queues.

Verbal manipulation of your opponent should be considered almost as important a skill as physical manipulation. And in today's litigious society, it would be a beneficial addition to any martial art.

As one extreme example:

One could be pummeling their opponent while shouting "Please, I don't want to fight." That verbal outburst would be heard by not only the opponent, but by witnesses. And, that may make a world of difference if the situation were brought before a court.

As a second example:

SGM Edmund K. Parker got so confident in his martial art skills that one time when he was confronted by a number of individuals, and before any physical actions occurred, he stopped and took the time to ask each one of the men how they would like to die in the confrontation. This so confounded and intimidated to the group that they backed down and the confrontation never occurred. Later Mr. Parker came up with the name for the *strategy*: "the menu of death." And in this situation, it worked and was the most *economical* outcome.

Physical

So, why do we care so much about the *economy of others*?

Because learning how to identify the use of *economy* (along with *efficiency* and *effectiveness*) in others, opens doors for manipulation, regulation, and exploitation.

Also, learning to use an opponent's energy and unique characteristics to aid in your own execution can, in turn, make your maneuvers more *economical* and potentially more *effective*. Analysis of the opponent and understanding how to use their movements to make your defensive / offensive actions more *economical* are a critical aspect of many martial arts.

A good example of noticing the (lack of) *economy* of others:

Almost everyone has witnessed or seen a fight were the combatants were wildly swinging at each other. And, as a trained martial artist, one would probably be thinking about how improper, wasteful and *ineffective* the motions were. And, maybe even how easy it would be to defeat them. Plus, if one watched the fight long enough, it wouldn't be surprising to see the combatants huffing and puffing from exhaustion within a relatively short period of time.

One important main thing to keep in mind with all this discussion, is that the sections and elements outlined in this chapter are only some of the primary aspects to examine and study. It is intended for the reader to use these deliberations as a starting point. A step in the right direction of your own analysis and discoveries.

Patterns

Patterns. People like and adhere to *patterns*. We are *pattern* junkies.

Why?

Because it's comfortable and easier - i.e. more *economical*.

For one, it builds muscle memory. It's a sure bet that just about every reader of this book can walk into a dark room in their home and turn on the light without much trouble at all; probably without looking or even really thinking about it. That's muscle memory. And muscle memory is a form of a *pattern*. Less effort and more *economy* through repetition until the exercise can be executed without much thought or expenditure of wasted energy.

And, a good portion of every martial art is built upon building muscle memory. Endless hours of practicing the same things over and over again. Perfection through repetitious practice. Strike, punch, kick, block: followed by forms (a.k.a. katas) and self-defense (a.k.a. one-step sparring).

The upside to this form of training is getting better through practice. The downside is building habits and patterns that can be exploited. And, potentially burning bad habits into muscle memory.

Ever try to cross train in a completely different type of martial art?

It can be very difficult. Learning to break habits and patterns that one has become comfortable with over years and potentially decades of training can be quite challenging. And again, that can be exploited.

> Note: There is an overlap with the **Fundamentals** chapter.

> Note: There is an overlap with the **Spontaneity** chapter.

Back to **patterns** in general. Essentially, **patterns** allow us to not use as much brain power to do something.

In other words, **patterns** can be more **economical** than randomness. **Patterns** allow us to free up brain energy (and potentially physical energy) for other things as we execute our specific **pattern**, primarily on auto-pilot.

But, the downside of **patterns** is that they are, by definition, predictable and therefore can be taken advantage of. Learn to recognize **patterns** in not only others, but yourself. And then develop methods to exploit them.

> Note: **Patterns** share many traits with **telegraphs**. And like **telegraphs**, **patterns** can change dramatically with the individual. Because of the similarities, **patterns** can often be analyzed simultaneously with **telegraphs**.
>
> One can think of **patterns** as a cousin to the **telegraphs** - or as a form of **telegraph**. And as such, should be treated in the same vein as the **telegraph**. For more information see the **Efficiency / Telegraphs** section of this chapter.

> Note: **Patterns** has a cousin concept; **if this then that**. For more information see the **if This Then That** section in the **Spontaneity** chapter.

> Note: There is an overlap with the **Effectiveness / Copying** section of this chapter.

As an exercise in recognizing **patterns**:

Take a day and go through it trying to recognize what patterns you have - no matter how small or insignificant. If done with earnest, one will probably find a vast number of *patterns* that they don't even know they were doing. But that is the norm.

Then as a follow up exercise:

Spend another day recognizing the *patterns* of all the people interacted with during that day.

> *Opinion: As a martial artist, one should always be aware of their* ***patterns*** *and learn how to control them and change them up at will. In other words, learn to be randomly* ***spontaneous*** *and unpredictable. At the same time, one should be able to quickly spot the* ***patterns*** *of others.*

Redirection

Redirection is the diverting of an opponent's movement in order to lessen, completely nullify, or reverse its intended effect. Redirection can be as simple as blocking or as complex as rerouting the opponent's energy back to them.

> *Note: **Redirection** is a reactive action. The opposite of this would be preventative action. Preventative action is a whole consideration in itself and is not considered here. See the **Economy of Yourself / Preventative vs Anticipatory** section of this chapter.*

Two examples of martial arts that realize *economy of self* through the use of energy of others are:

Judo and Aikido.

Both of these martial arts use their opponent's energy against them in an *efficient* manner for the practitioner. One of the primary tenants of both martial arts is to be as *economical* as possible, while simultaneously taking advantage of the energy expended by the opponent.

> *In contrast to **borrowed force**:*
>   * ***redirection*** *is a less destructive and more defensive*
>   * ***redirection*** *will typically use circular patterns*

Borrowing Force

As mentioned previously in this chapter, use of the opponent's physical force in *redirection* can be a very *effective* means of both defense and offense. But there is still a more *effective* means of offense - direct opposition to the opponent's force in order to enhance your offensive action.

> Note: **Borrowed force** should be thought of as using your opponent's motion to enhance both the *efficiency* and *effectiveness* of your maneuvers.

> Note: There is an overlap with the *Effectiveness /Opposing Forces*. section of this chapter.

To use an example of how this tool works:

Imagine a truck hitting an in-penetrable wall at 50mph: there would be a lot of damage to the truck. Now imagine that same truck, moving at the same speed, having a direct head on collision with the exact same truck coming at it at 50mph. The collision would be double; or 100mph.

Other ways to look at this scenario:

In order to get the same damage as the first collision, the first truck doesn't even need to be moving. Or, both trucks only need to be moving at 25mph.

In other words, the truck would get the same damage with far less speed, if the object it was hitting was moving toward it. Thus, the term *borrowed force*. From the first truck's *perspective*, if it borrows the force from the second truck, it could do same damage, but be more *economical* in the force it delivers to the scenario - yet the resulting damage would be the same.

*Note: The **opposite** should also be considered here. The reason why points are not typically scored in a martial arts tournament when an opponent (or defender) is moving away from a strike is for the **opposite** reason. The force of the impact will be lessened considerably and therefore not considered a knockout blow.*

*In contrast to **redirection**:*
        * ***borrowed force*** is more destructive and more offensive
        * ***borrowed force*** will typically use linear patterns

*Note: In American Kenpo lingo, this act is referred to as **borrowed force** (and should not be confused with **opposing forces**).*

Economy of the Environment

As discussed in the chapter on *environment*, *environment* is anything that is: in, on, or around you. Using the *environment* for the purpose of *economy*, once expressed, seems very obvious and logical. And, many of these environmental aspects are discussed in other parts of this chapter.

Therefore, this section will limit its discussion to things around you, excluding your opponent - i.e. what we typically refer to as our *environment*. Some things that fall into this category are; walls, chairs, tables, doors, steps, floor, etc.

> *Note: One may not see the floor as a weapon, but slamming the opponent to the floor, as opposed to just letting the opponent fall (from say a sweep), should be considered.*

> *Note: Moving an opponent into an environmental weapon to cause damage is the opposite of hitting the opponent with a (non-physical) weapon (e.g. knife, stick, etc.). In American Kenpo lingo this topic can be referred to as: target to weapon / weapon to target.*

Just like *non-physical weapons*, one's surroundings can be used to not only enhance the *effectiveness* of specific maneuvers, but also to aid in the *economy* of maneuvers. Using the hardness of our modern-day surroundings can allow one to be far more *economical* in defensive and offensive execution.

> *Note: Use of **environment** goes hand-in-hand with **redirection** and **borrowed force**. In the case of **borrowed force**, the **environment** is not always fixed and can itself be moved and used to injure a moving opponent.*

Something to consider with the *environment*, but can be used across a variety of circumstances: There are three scenarios that can occur:

1) the opponent hits the **environment**.

2) the **environment** hits the opponent.

3) both hit each other.

> *Note: There is a fourth scenario that is not called out: the nothing scenario - i.e. the opponent and the* ***environment*** *don't hit. This would be the most common scenario, since most of the time we don't use our* ***environment*** *as a weapon.*

Another thing to consider is that not only can the **environment** be used as a weapon to aid in **economy**, it can also be used in other ways for **economy**.

For example:

If one were riding a bike and hit someone, would one even have to throw the punch? Or, just extend their arm/hand out? If one jumped off the stairs and kicked someone, are they really kicking, or just holding their leg out and letting gravity do all the work? If one vaulted (not jumped) over a chair to kick someone, could they kick higher, if it was necessary?

All examples of using the **environment** in **economical** ways to one's advantage.

> *Note: This section has an overlap with the chapter on* ***Consideration Priority****: For instance: If the opponent was on the other side of a locked door, does one even have to do anything? Or, if the opponent was tied up or being held back by his friends, what is actually required? In other words, how does the environmental situation effect the* ***economy*** *of one's response.*

Economy vs Conservation

With all of this discussion of *economy*, the reader should not get it confused with *conservation*. They are similar, but distinctly different *strategies*. Where *economy* seeks to optimize the use of energy, *conservation* flips *economy* on its head (*opposite*) and actively tries to avoid using energy.

In other words, *conservation* is the active and purposeful avoidance of energy use, where *economy* is the management of energy already being used.

Conservation typically comes from the *perspective* that we all have a limited energy resource (and sometimes depleted). And, it seeks to actively minimize energy consumption.

A rude, but true reality is that we all have physical limits. Probably many readers of this book have sparred on occasion to the point of near exhaustion, making it very difficult to punch, kick, defend, wrestle, roll, etc. very *effectively*. This is one point where *conservation* starts to become obvious as a *strategy*.

A good example of a famous *conservation* tactic:

Muhammad Ali's "rope-a-dope" *strategy*. This is where he actively taunted his opponent to aggressively attack him, while he primarily defended himself. He knowingly did this with the understanding that the opponent was consuming a lot of energy and would eventually begin to tire, while Ali would stay safe by being overly defensive - conserving energy. But then at the right time, Ali would turn the tables on a fatigued opponent, for the victory.

Another good example of *conservation* in action:

M.M.A. fighters that are mounted by an opponent will often just relax and not resist the opponent on top of them. But rather, they will only exert enough energy as to not be hurt or moved into a compromising position. Only when the fighter sees an available opening will they then exert the needed force to escape or counter the opponent.

And finally, a martial art that's entirely built upon the *strategy* of *conservation* is Systema. It comes from the *perspective* that the practitioner starts in a potentially weakened (starving or injured) state and needs to exert as little energy as possible in order to defend and/or defeat an opponent - often using absorption, deflection, deceptive and/or disruptive distance changes and *timings* to achieve its goals. All with the least possible amount of energy expenditure.

Efficiency

In this section, *efficiency* will primarily concentrate on eliminating wasted and/or ineffective motion when performing actions and maneuvers; specifically, in the context of the martial arts. *Efficiency* could also be used with eliminating wasted power, but that responsibility will be delegated to the section on *economy*.

In other words, for the purpose of this chapter; *efficiency* is the recognition and removal of action that is unneeded or ineffective for its intended purpose.

Based upon the previous statements, probably the first thing one should understand is that *efficiency* doesn't exclusively translate to the distance (a) maneuver(s) travel(s) or the time it takes to accomplish the maneuver(s), although those are probably the most prominent and obvious factors of *efficiency*. *Efficiency* can translate to many other characteristics of (a) maneuver(s); such as *intent* or *method*.

Economy, Efficiency, and Effectiveness 103

Distance and Time

So, let's get the most obvious elements of *efficiency* out of the way - *distance* and *time*.

The first thing to notice about these two (2) characteristics and their association to *efficiency* is that they are considerably related to one another. For the most part, one could say a shorter *distance* translates to lesser *time*. And, one major way to achieve quicker *time* is through a shorter *distance*. Very straight forward and pretty much indisputable.

So, we are done, right?

Well, no.

There are other issues that the above analysis does not consider. Such as:

Is the shorter *distance* obstructed? Does the position we are currently executing the maneuver from (as *efficiently* as possible) diminish its *effectiveness*? Am I even able to use the most *efficient* path at all from my current positioning?

So, just because there is a more *efficient* way, it doesn't always mean we can take advantage of it.

In other words, it breaks the part of the definition "competency in performance."

For instance:

Is it more *efficient* to repeatedly pump a linear punch with a single hand, or circle the hand in a figure eight (8) pattern to strike repeatedly?

Notice the question and your answer. Some may have said:

Definitely the figure eight (8).

Others might have said:

But the linear punch is probably more *effective*.

Who's right?

It depends. No one can argue that the figure eight (8) is generally more *efficient*. But, was that the purpose of our action - to be as *efficient* as possible?

The above examination also dispels with following question:

If we are trying to be as *efficient* as possible, why isn't all motion linear?

It is the most *efficient* and therefore the quickest. It is true that linear motion is, by definition, the quicker of the two (2) types of motions (circular and linear). But that fact ignores the real world. And in the real world, there are a multitude of other factors that need to be considered.

> Note: There is an overlap with the section *Consideration Priority* of the *Principles and Rules* chapter.

To add more fuel to the mental fire; up to now, we've only concerned ourselves with *efficiency* of a single maneuver from a single weapon. But we have a host of weapons we can employ from various parts of our body, in an almost endless array of sequences.

In other words, we started to lose the forest through a single tree. The moral is:

Sometimes *efficiency* comes from the total, not the single. And, although *distance* and *time* are relevant and important factors to achieving *efficiency*, they are not the only factors to consider.

Cocking

Cocking can be described as repositioning a weapon away from its intended target, prior to delivery of a future maneuver.

The description probably has most readers thinking that *cocking* doesn't sound like a good idea. It adds more *time*, plus all the motion away from the target is wasted, because, by definition, it doesn't seem to be helping the execution of the maneuver. And on top of that, all the distance away from the target has to be recovered, so in essence, doubling the amount of travel of the weapon (at least for the *cocking* portion).

Wow, that all sounds bad! So, why do we do it?

Let's be honest, we all *cock* our weapons, at least some of the time.

Most everyone already instinctively knows the answer to the above question:

Distance is required to make the execution of the weapon more *effective*.

In other words, if the weapon is too close to the target, it may need to be *cocked* to be *effective*.

Our natural tendency is to get as much travel to a weapon as possible, with the unconscious (or conscience) understanding that it will help with speed (and ultimately power). Otherwise, the strike might not be able to have the desired effect.

But, *time* (and *efficiency*) pays the price for *cocking* the weapon. So, one might ask, why is this so bad?

There is a very simple rebuttal; in a lot of instances, more *time* between strikes translates into giving the opponent the opportunity to insert their own weapon(s) into the *time* gap.

In short, that *time* gap can be the difference between success and failure.

> Note: There is an overlap with the **Economy of Yourself / Physical** section of this chapter.

> Note: There is an overlap with section **Effectiveness / Timing** section of this chapter.

So, two (2) important questions arise from the above discussion:

1) How much distance is a good enough distance?

2) Is there a way to get both distance without affecting *efficiency* in *time*?

First, how much distance? This is a subjective one, because there is no real answer - it all depends upon one's training, and their skill level.

As discussed in another section, some very skilled people need hardly any *distance* to be *effective*. So, only the reader themself can really answer this question. But, that answer can change with training and ability.

It is most probable that one's *distance* requirements have lessened since they first started training in the martial arts. This may be the best one will ever be, or one may decide more training is required or desired to further improve on this requirement.

> Note: There is an overlap with the **method** section of this chapter.

Some readers may be saying:

This all sounds like you're just throwing the problem into my lap. Is there a way we overcome the difficulties of the first question and get the distance without the *time* gap?

Yes. The answer lies in not concentrating on the weapon in question, but rather the body as a whole.

Let's consider the following example:

What if, one needed to **cock** a weapon, and as they did it, they inserted another strike from another limb at the same time as the **cocking** of the first weapon; specifically, to fill the gap. Problem solved.

Another interesting tidbit about this **strategy**, one should consider:

The inserted strike could be a maneuver not designed to knock-out the opponent, but rather, intended to keep them busy or distracted while the primary weapon is repositioned.

This all sounds much easier that the first answer; and it is, but just like the first answer, it requires skill - just a different kind.

> Note: Given the example above; in American Kenpo lingo, the secondary strike would be called a minor strike, while the primary strike would be called a major strike. Also, the secondary strike could be referred to as an insert.

Some very important things to take away from the above discussion:

a) One should be aware of their own **cocking** habits and its effect on **efficiency**.

b) How those gaps in **efficiency** can be exploited.

c) How to spot and exploit the **cocking** habits of others.

> Note: There is an overlap with the **Economy / Economy of Others / Physical / Patterns** section of this chapter.

A highly recommended exercise to do:

Video yourself executing maneuvers - maybe sparring or some form of self-defense techniques. And, then watch yourself to see if you can spot any unintentional *cocking* of weapons. This can include leaning (for kicks), definite *cocking* of weapons, or very slight or almost imperceptible movements prior to executing a maneuver.

Next, take the time to correct these issues.

And finally, repeat this exercise occasionally to see if any unintended movements creep back into your technique.

> *Note: One can also use this same exercise to help in learning to analyze the motions of others.*

> *Note: There is an overlap with the **Telegraphs** section of this chapter.*

So, now that we've discussed re-positioning of the weapon to get more travel, let's flip that idea on it's head (*opposite* again).

There are a couple of things that were purposely overlooked and not stated above:

1) We are not in a static fighting situation.

In other words, the defender and the opponent are not always stationary in a combat situation, and this can be exploited.

2) There are other reasons to *cock* a weapon than just for *distance* of travel, such as; alignment of muscles, better body placement, etc. (i.e. improved positioning).

By now, some readers may be pondering:

This is all true and sounds great, but what in the world does this have to do with *opposites*?

This is where it gets interesting - there are more elements in this equation that just the weapon one needs to *cock*.

For instance:

Instead of moving the weapon, move the body (leaving the weapon fixed in space). Or, instead of moving yourself, move your opponent. And, even more; how about moving all (or any combination) of the above: weapon, body, and/or your opponent.

One's mind should begin to race with all sorts of ideas! This type of thinking changes everything! This paradigm is so powerful and now clearly obvious that no more examples are really needed.

But, as an exercise:

Take the time to explore these possibilities. The door is now open, walk through it and explore the other side.

> Note: In American Kenpo lingo, moving the body while leaving the weapon fixed in space for the purpose of **cocking** the weapon is referred to as spatial **cocking**.

> Note: There is an overlap with the **Opposites and Reverses** chapter.

Intent

So, what is *intent*? Why is it important? And, what does it have to do with *efficiency*?

Intent can be succinctly described as the purpose behind action.

For example:

If one where to see another practitioner in a fighting stance and watch them deliver a vertical forearm maneuver; how would they interpret that maneuver? Is it defensive (a block)? Or, is it offensive (a strike)?

There may be some physical clues, such as speed or intensity that may give one a hint. But, probably the only real way to get a full understanding of the maneuver might be to ask the practitioner what their *intent* was.

OK that was easy, but what does *intent* have to do with *efficiency*?

Well, *intent* is not entirely limited to totally defensive or offensive maneuvering. Sometimes it has other purposes, such as; distracting, redirecting attention, body (re)positioning, signaling, or directing. So, what otherwise might be interpreted as not *efficient* from the standpoint of purely defensive or offensive maneuvering, could otherwise be completely *efficient*, given the *intent* of the action.

For example:

If one were to watch an opponent open and close their hand, they might interpret this as meaningless or in-*efficient* and/or in-*effective* motion. But the opponent's ultimate *intent* may have been to distract their rival into looking at the hand.

From that understanding, the motion was completely *efficient* in both movement and purpose.

> Note: There is an overlap with the **Mind / Strategy and Theory** section of **The Human Element** chapter.

Some readers may have caught the previous implication.

Notice the last part of the previous sentence: "*efficient* in both movement and purpose." This statement correctly implies that *efficiency* is not only limited to physical maneuvers, but can also be applied to the non-physical. And, in order to be *efficient* in non-physical ways, a clear understanding of *intent* is required.

This example shows that what otherwise might be interpreted as completely useless, unwarranted or wasted; with a new understanding of *intent*, changes to completely useful, skillful, and clever.

> Note: There is an overlap with the **Effectiveness**, **Telegraphs**, **Baiting**, and **Copying** sections of this chapter.

Method

There were a least a few readers, after reading the beginning of this section, saying to themselves:

Method? What's that?

For our purposes, *method* can roughly be described as how motions travel through space and time.

That probably helps a little, but an example is probably in order:

A good example, due to the obvious differences (*opposites*), is: staccato vs continuous motion.

Staccato motion is motion that stops and starts between maneuvers or within the maneuver. These maneuvers tend to have a pause or delay (however small) somewhere during their delivery.

Continuous motion is motion that has no gap in *timing* (or pause in speed) between multiple maneuvers.

Staccato and continuous can be described as different *methods* of executing the maneuvers.

In other words, the way in which the maneuvers are performed is different. And, these different *methods* apply to both singular and multiple maneuver sequences.

> Note: Circular maneuvers tend to be more continuous (e.g. figure eight [8]). Linear maneuvers tend to be more staccato.

To examine this further:

Imagine executing punches from a training stance. There are basically two major ways to execute these punches:

1) Each punch is executed and then returned to the starting point and then the next punch is executed and also returned to the starting point.

2) Each punch is executed and then returned to the starting point with the execution of the next punch.

Of these two approaches, which is the most *efficient*?

The correct answer is; It depends. Are we considering each punch independently of each other, or as a sequence? Are we talking about *efficiency* of time? All this and more effects the answer.

If we are considering each punch independently of each other, then each punch is as *efficient* as it is intended to be.

In other words, neither option is the better choice.

But, if we are considering them as a sequence and *efficiency* of time is our top priority, then option number two (2) is the correct answer.

At this point, some readers might be asking them-self:

So what? Why is this stuff important?

It is important because it is imperative that one understands that where boundaries and priorities are drawn, when considering *efficiency* is critical to the analysis. Analyzing the *efficiency* of a single maneuver is completely different than for a sequence of maneuvers.

And, it is crucial to understand that *efficiency* may affect a number of other factors; such as *timing*, *intent*, and *effectiveness*. And, this effect can be positive or negative.

And furthermore, the negative effect may be more important than the *efficiency* gains.

As a simple example of how *efficiency* of a single weapon, it's *method* of execution, and *effectiveness* are all intertwined:

Let's examine a single, straight punch to the opponent's face.

We could possibly make the maneuver more *efficient* by compounding this maneuver with an elbow to the face, with the same limb.

Two for one, more *efficient*, right?

Sure, but how does that effect other factors? Did compounding the elbow take away from the *effectiveness* of the punch?

Quite possibly, if one were concentrating on delivering the elbow and not the punch.

Or, what about if the distance wasn't proper for the *effective* execution of both strikes.

In other words, if the punch were jammed, or if the gap was too big for delivering a proper elbow.

Each of these factors not only effect *efficiency*, but also *effectiveness*.

And, this type of exploration only gets more complex as one moves from single maneuvers to sequences of maneuvers.

So, to sum this all up:

Small changes in how maneuvers are executed can have an effect on *efficiency*. But, these adjustments also can have ripple effects to other elements in both positive and negative ways.

So, one should always be sure to that they have a good understanding of their priorities when dealing with this type of analysis and how changes in *method* effect the other factors of the whole.

Note: This discussion has an overlap with the chapter on ***Consideration Priority***.

Telegraphs

Telegraphing (a.k.a. tell) can be roughly defined as the recognition of action before it occurs based upon physical queues.

In other words, reading and using changes, no matter how subtle or minute, in your opponent to figure out what they are going to do; before they actually do it.

Most people have "tells". Many card gamblers make their entire careers upon recognizing and taking advantage of "tells". Martial arts are no different. Quickly recognizing and learning how to take advantage of an opponent's *telegraph*(s) is an entire skill and art in and of itself.

One thing to keep in mind is that taking advantage of a tell could be for either defensive or offensive (or a combination of both) purposes.

> *Note: Sometimes a **telegraph** can be lack or modification of movement. One case to consider is when an opponent has continuous or **patterned** movement by default; but alters, or stops, the movement prior to their intended movement(s).*

The major thing to understand is that *telegraphs* are all based upon physical movement of some sort. It can be as subtle as a change in expression or as obvious as *cocking* a weapon before delivery.

One of the best venues to explore and analyze *telegraphing* is sparring. Practicing the recognition of *telegraphing* during sparring sessions can be a very valuable exercise that can then be transferred to other aspects of the martial arts. And, the more individuals one spars, the better their skills in recognition will become.

This is because different people will have wildly different tells. And, learning to analyze and explore the many ways to take advantage of each cannot be understated.

Needless to say, becoming an expert in understanding and taking advantage of *telegraphs* is a complex, yet valuable skill that should be scrutinized extensively.

> *Note: **Telegraphs** share many traits with **patterns**. And like **patterns**, **telegraphs** can change dramatically with the individual. Because of the similarities, **telegraphs** can often be analyzed simultaneously with **patterns**.*

It is worth repeating that it is important to recognize that *telegraphs* are frequently very small physical motions or may be audible. An opponent may grunt, hold their breath, change expression, change prior motion, slightly *cock* a weapon, lean, or settle their stance just prior to or along with their intended maneuver(s).

There are various ways to deal with telegraphs ranging from defensive to offensive. But, one outstanding *strategy* is preemption.

In other words, beat the opponent's action with your own. If the opponent signals they are about to do something; disrupt, confound, or prevent their action with your own. This tends to be a good course of action because it not only cancels out their maneuver, but it also hides the fact that their tell is recognized.

In short, more *efficient* and *effective* along with being deceptive.

To improve on this *strategy* further, one shouldn't always use the same preemptive measure. If changed up, it will be harder for the opponent to figure out that they are being read.

For instance:

One should pick and choose when they will let the opponent execute their maneuver and when they will tamper with it. And, when tampering is done, it should be done with a variety of countermeasures.

> Note: There is an overlap with the **If This Then That** section of the **Spontaneity** chapter.

Another thing to consider with **telegraphs** is that what might be interpreted as a **telegraph**, might be a means of distraction, redirection, or **baiting**. A glance at something, a verbal queue, or a physical anomaly could be used to elicit a response.

So, one's job is to ignore the distractions and zero in on the real **telegraphs**.

And finally, if the opponent uses the same technique(s) over and over with the **intent** to distract or redirect attention, that maneuver can also be re-purposed as a **telegraph**.

> Note: There is overlap with the sections **Intent**, **Baiting**, and **Copying** in this chapter.

Effectiveness

In this section, *effectiveness* will concentrate on improving and/or maximizing results of actions and maneuvers; specifically, in the context of the martial arts.

In other words, *effectiveness* is getting the best results one can from their actions.

If one stops to think about it, martial arts is basically learning to eliminate ineffective movements and actions, while simultaneously learning to perform preplanned reactions and maneuvers, specifically for the purpose of self-defense. But, how many of us martial artists stop to look at the movements we've learned and actually analyzed whether they are executed as *effectively* as possible.

The prior statement brings up the following questions:

What is meant by *effectively* as possible? Didn't we all learn the maneuvers *effectively* when they were taught to us?

Maybe yes: maybe no. Depends upon both the student and the instructor who taught the maneuvers.

Regardless, do we actually stop to look at our maneuvers, break them down to their basic elements and analyze whether we have maximized their *effectiveness*?

Probably not.

Frequently, small adjustments to how a maneuver is executed can make a large difference in *effectiveness*. Sometimes the adjustment may be as small as dropping an elbow a half of an inch, adjusting an angle of delivery by a few degrees, or other *nuanced* body alterations.

> *Opinion: If you have not taken the time to honestly analyze yourself and your maneuvers for **effectiveness**, you are doing yourself an injustice.*

> *Note: There is an overlap with the chapter on **Nuance**.*

Please keep in mind what is NOT being said here:

This discussion is not about the reader's specific martial art being **effective** of ineffective, but rather about whether YOU are actually executing the maneuvers you already know and do as **effectively** as possible - by you.

Any of us can develop bad habits, misinterpret execution, or have not been corrected about a misalignment we picked up during our years of training. It is very easy for any of us to not be fully self-aware and not see issues that have arisen over time within ourselves. Especially, if one is a head instructor or doesn't have anyone to critically and dispassionately observe them and give critical feedback.

A good exercise:

Video yourself doing your martial arts. Then stop to look at the video from the **perspective** of you being the instructor of yourself and give yourself feedback of what you would do to make yourself better and more **effective**.

In short, learn to be your own instructor. Treat yourself like you would treat your favorite student. The one you want to make the best they can be. Be tough on yourself.

> *Note: There is an overlap here with the chapters on **Rationalization**, **Perspective**, and **Opposites and Reverses**.*

Another way to look at it is:

We are all humans, and as such, we are all subject to making mistakes.

Therefore, learn to be your own biggest detractor, learn to be and stay more self-aware and critical of yourself; rather than more content and less aware of your own movements and thoughts over time (opposite). Time adds valuable experience, seasoning, and confidence; but it also can allow for more bad habits and complacency to creep in and potentially detract from your effectiveness. Don't allow for this to happen.

Further Exploration

Martial arts training can generally be described as learning to eliminate and/or minimize the in-*effective* and maximize the *effective* in relation to self-defense and conflict.

As such, one should not *categorize* maneuvers and/or *strategies* as useless or useful; rather one should think of such things as being in-*effective* or *effective*.

Why?

Because in-*effective* does not have the same negative mental impact as useless. And, sometimes in-*effective* factors and aspects can be made more *effective* with modifications or under specific circumstances.

But, something that is useless tends to stay useless, mentally.

> *Factoid/Opinion: A little known fact from the annals of martial arts history: the back-knuckle strike was not considered a point in tournament competition until the late '50's to early '60's. Why? Because it wasn't considered effective enough to knock-out an opponent, and therefore deemed not a point. It wasn't until a martial art's master proved the back-knuckle could knock-out an opponent (by doing so) that it was approved as a point in competition. Contrast that to what is considered a point today in tournaments. How far we have come.*

One thing that can't be ignored when it comes to *effectiveness*: human anatomy. There are just some movements that a human can't perform *effectively*.

For example:

Let's look at a simple block executed in front of the body. With the fist pointing upward, there are four (4) possible blocks - 2 with the fist facing generally toward the body; 2 with the fist facing generally away from the body.

How many of these possibilities are *effective*?

Well, there is one (1) that would be considered in-*effective*. The one that moves toward the center with the palm facing away from the body.

Now, let's do that same with the hand pointing downward.

There is also one (1) that would be considered in-*effective*: the one that moves away from the center with the palm facing upward.

So out of the eight (8) possible combinations, six (6) would be considered *effective* and two (2) wouldn't.

In other words, 75% are effective, 25% are in-*effective*.

So, what do we do with the two (2) in-*effective* blocks?

We *classify* them as in-*effective* and omit them from our training.

> Note: In American Kenpo lingo, the exclusion of specific moves like the ones describe above is called *purposeful omission*.

> Note: There is an overlap with the chapter on **Organization, Classification, and Categorization**.

As an exercise:

Take the time to go through the example presented above with many other *categories* of maneuvers. While this is being done, also take the time to *classify* which maneuvers are purposely not executing in your training. It can be very fascinating to study the limits of our own anatomical make-up and explore why we martial artists exclude specific maneuvers and include others.

And even further, why we all tend to prefer a relatively small set of possible maneuvers.

Another thing one should uncover if they perform the exercise presented, is that there is not always an yeah or nay with maneuvers. To be more accurate, one should find that there is actually a *spectrum* of *effectiveness*.

Note: There is an overlap with the **Spectrum** section of the **Opposites and Reverses** chapter.

And on top of that, *effectiveness* can change based upon a number of factors, such as; weapon hardness to target hardness, part of body used (e.g. head vs hand), how the maneuver is executed, from what starting position the weapon is executed, etc.

For example:

Throwing a punch while the hand is extended above the head is far less *effective* than dropping the fist downward and hitting with the side of the fist (i.e. a hammer-fist). But the same can't be said with the same fist at chest level and then thrusting forward to strike.

One major factor that influences *effectiveness* and is covered more comprehensively in its own chapter, is the *environment*. But, suffice it to say that what may be completely *effective* in one *environment* is not as *effective* in another. And, sometimes is completely in-*effective*.

Simply put, *environment* is so important to all that we do, it was given its own chapter.

> *Note: Keep in mind that up to now we have only dealt with a single maneuver. This analysis can be further extrapolated to multiple maneuvers.*

So, there is one major question that needs to be addressed at this point:

Can we be too effective? In other words, can what I am doing do more than what I intended?

Simply put, yes. And, although in a lot of the cases that can be a good thing, some of the cases that is a bad thing.

Take the following extreme example:

One is being attacked by an opponent and their *intention* is to knock them out with a punch. But, they are so effective that they accidentally kill them. Is that a problem? Legally, it very well could be.

> *Note: There is an overlap with the **Efficiency/Intent** section of this chapter.*

Now a slightly less extreme example:

One has a *strategy* where the same attacker is moving toward them. Their *intention* is to stop the opponent's forward momentum with a kick so that they can then be defeated with upper body maneuvers (i.e. punches, elbows, etc.). But the kick sends them sailing backward instead. Problem? Very well could be. At the very least, the *strategy* will definitely have to change.

> *Note: There is an overlap with the **Mind/Strategy and Theory** section of **The Human Element** chapter.*

The moral to the above:

One should make sure they are as *effective* as they need to be for the situation and *strategy*. Just like less, more can also be a problem.

Keep this in mind in not only this section, but also in other areas of this book.

Opposing Forces

Let's openly admit something to ourselves right now, we can only become so *effective*. There is a limit. And once we have reached that limit, one could ask - is there more?

Well, what if one could develop and use power in multiple directions at the same time and in such a way that they work together to make more of an impact than if used separately.

> Note: There is an overlap with the **Economy/Economy of Others/Physical/Borrowing Force** section of this chapter.

For example:

After delivering a strike, how about if we use the pulling power of the retracting weapon to pull the opponent into a pushing type strike of a follow up weapon. The pulling could be done in such a way as to further enhance the power of the pushing strike, making it's impact more *effective*. This could be done any number of ways using any combination of upper body and lower body strikes.

> Note: In American Kenpo lingo, this act is referred to as **opposing forces** (and should not be confused with **borrowed force**).

> Note/Opinion: This type of maneuvering can become very important to smaller and/or weaker individuals against a larger opponent.

> Note: There is an overlap with the **Efficiency/Distance and Time/Cocking** section of this chapter.

As suggested above, we often must *cock* and/or re-position our weapons after they are used offensively. Most of the time, that travel is not being used to its fullest potential and therefore the energy already being expended is, in effect, being wasted. That is travel and power we don't often think about. But, we should.

> *Note/Opinion:* **Opposing forces** *should be thought of as using your own, wasted energy to aid in enhancing the* **effectiveness** *of your maneuvers.*

As an exercise:

Go through some maneuvers that are often practiced or taught. Take the time to discover and explore the motions that might fall into this *category* of 'wasted motion'. Then, take the time to see which maneuvers could potentially be easily modified to make it more *effective*.

> *Note: There is an overlap with the chapter on* **Organization, Classification, and Categorization.**

So, the above discourse may elicit the following question:

Do we have to have directly *opposing forces*?

In short, no. But, as the directions become less aligned, so does the ability to enhance our follow-up maneuver.

In other words, the less the forces are in opposition, the more they are moving in concert with each other; until perpendicular. Beyond perpendicular, the other motion is taking away from the *effectiveness* of our maneuver (*opposite*).

Why?

Because now both motions are starting to move in the same relative direction.

In summary, one can take advantage of any motions that are moving in relative opposition to one another at any opposing angle. But the closer one gets to the motions being in direct opposition, the more *effective* this *strategy* will become.

Gravitation Constant

Now, let's turn this concept on this head a little and answer this obvious, but often overlooked question:

Is there another force that, like the motions mentioned previously, is frequently not exploited to make our maneuvers as *effective* as they could be?

Well, yes. In a simple word, gravity.

Could we then use gravity to make our maneuvers more *effective*?

Absolutely!

But, how?

Well, what do we know about gravity?

First, the most obvious thing is it is always pulling us down. Therefore, if we are moving up and down in our movements, we use gravity to help make our maneuvers more *effective*.

> *Note: There is an overlap with the **Alignment** section of this chapter.*

> *Note: In American Kenpo lingo, this **strategy** is referred to as gravitational marriage (a.k.a. marriage with gravity).*

With the above statements, the following rebuttal could potentially be made:

OK, but one is not often doing maneuvers up and down! So, there is a limited amount of opportunity for anyone to use gravity.

Not true. Just because maneuvers are primarily done on a horizontal plane (i.e. parallel to the ground). That doesn't mean that one can't add a small element of vertical motion to the maneuver and let gravity help make the maneuver more *effective* (and *efficient*).

To clarify this response further, an example is definitely in order:

Imagine one is in their favorite fighting stance and they deliver a punch straight ahead to their opponent's mid-section. Let's assume it is perfectly parallel to the floor. It's strong, powerful, and beautiful.

What could make it better?

How about if they settled their weight just a bit and made a small re-direction of the punch to a very slight downward angle, all exactly *timed* so that all the different forces are in harmony and enhance each-other.

Wouldn't it be logical that the use of gravity would have made the strike more *effective*?

Even if it was only by 5% or 10%. That is more power generated than without the use of gravity.

Are we willing to give that up? Only you can answer this question.

> Note: In American Kenpo lingo, the dropping of the weight (and height) slightly is referred to as settling your stance.

> Note: There is an overlap with the **Timing** section of this chapter.

To circle this discussion back around to the previous section; just like *opposing forces*, as the angle of delivery of the maneuver gets further from parallel to the ground, the more potential effect gravity can have on that maneuver.

In other words, the more diagonal the motion, the more powerful the effect of gravity is and can be used toward **effectiveness**.

And as always, one should take the time to figure out what else this **strategy** can be applied to.

And, to put one final twist question into the mental mix:

Can one take advantage of gravity in some way going upward (**opposite**)?

This is left as an exercise for the reader to ponder and explore. (Hint: yes - think Newton [and **alignment**]).

> Note: Just to point something out: in space (and in micro-gravity situations), almost everything about this discourse changes.

> Note: Another way to look at this is; **opposing forces** should be thought of as **effectiveness** of self, **borrowed force** as **effectiveness** of self through the use others, and the use of gravity as **effectiveness** of self through the use of **environment**.
>
> The chapters **Perspective** and **Environment** may help in adding more context and further clarification to this statement.

Timing

There is a famous joke that goes:

Timing......is everything.

Timing goes by many different names; synchronization, coordination, and harmony to name a few common ones.

Timing is so important that without it nothing works; but with it, everything works.

Very bold statement - some readers may be thinking. A bit of embellishment and overstatement - some others are definitely thinking.

But, stop for a moment and really ponder what that statement says and means.

For instance, without proper *timing* any defense, offense, step or even breath one takes will not work. But with it, they all work.

OK great, *timing* is important.

Stop! That is not what is being said here. What is being said is - *timing* is everything.

This is worth repeating again - *TIMING* IS EVERYTHING!

Has it sunk in yet?

Hopefully. Now we can proceed forward.

For example:

If one were to stop and go over all their martial arts training, from the beginning, what were they learning to do?

In essence, they were learning two (2) things:

1) How to understand combat and its *strategies*, in the context of their specific martial art.

2) How to coordinate them-self properly to physically express the *mental* aspects of what they learned in their martial art.

In other words, how to think properly and how to move properly; as an expression of their martial art.

The point being, all that movement (and thought) is the result of proper *timing*.

> *Note: There is an overlap with the chapters* **Nuance,** **Fundamentals,** *and* **The Human Element.**

This is definitely all very heady stuff, but you are the one that decided to read this book. So please, take the time to really stop and dwell on what is being said in this section. Try and consider all the avenues that a commanding knowledge and mindfulness of *timing* opens up. It is pretty much guaranteed that everyone reading this won't find them all, but they will find more and more with gained experience and with continued further thought and exploration.

Yes, this subject is that vast, and that important.

> *Note: Some more topics in this book that may help when first starting to explore these avenues of exploration into* *timing are:* **Opposites and Reverses, Perspective,** *and* **Spontaneity,**

Skipping a Beat

The previous section alluded to the fact that all one is doing in their training is learning proper *timing*. And, from a very high-level *perspective* that is true.

But, isn't *timing* of multiple elements a form of a *pattern*? And, with all *patterns* can't they be predicted and taken advantage of?

In short, yes. And as such, we must be very cognizant of this fact.

> *Note: There is an overlap with the **Economy/Economy of Others/Physical/Patterns** section of this chapter.*

Stop and think about the above statements for a moment. If everything we are doing is just a bunch of *patterns* (a.k.a. *timing*), and if someone can recognize and disrupt the *pattern*, doesn't that *strategy* basically screw everything up?

In a word, yes.

For example:

One of the primary tenants of the martial art Systema is to disrupt the opponent's *timing* in such a way as to disrupt, confound, and potentially use the opponent's *timing* against them.

This is done by understanding the basic physical *timings* of specific maneuvers and learning where key disruptions in that coordination can cause catastrophic results to the intended maneuver. Sounds *effective*. And, it can be. But, understanding that *strategy* is also the answer to overcoming it.

How?

By changing the *pattern*.

Whoa: Hold on! Are you saying to change the *timing* of all the stuff I spent my entire training learning how to do right in the first place?

Yes.

Everyone probably does something similar to this frequently anyway, but for a different reason. How many times have we all delayed or sped up a maneuver in order to get to a target and defy an opponent and their defenses?

Probably, all the time. So, to carry this line of thought further:

If one can do it for a specific maneuver within a series of maneuvers, can't they do it for the elements within a single maneuver?

Exercise:

Take the time to understand the all *timing* that goes into specific maneuvers (one at a time). One should discover that there are more elements than they might have thought at first.

Next, take the time to explore how one can alter these *timings* and what that does to the maneuver itself.

Suffice it to be said, this knowledge and exercise can be used to open up more avenues than one might think or realize at first.

As a start in how to perform the above exercise:

Let's take a simple example and walk through some of the elements to consider.

Imagine standing in a left fighting stance, throwing a right straight punch directly ahead (a.k.a. a reverse punch). Whether it returns or not is up to the reader. The import part is to understand what elements made the punch possible and how they needed to work together to make it successful.

For instance, when did the punch rotate so that the palm faced downward; in the beginning, during the execution, or at the very end of the travel?

And, to get more detailed, what muscles of the arm made that rotation possible and when were they engaged?

OK, let's move to the shoulder and repeat. Then to the core of your body. And, then down to the leg.

Was the weight shifted forward slightly, or not? Did the hip rotate before the punch, during the punch, or at the end of the punch, or not at all? Why? And, what muscles were needed to perform this motion, if any? Did they tighten at all? When?

Now repeat this with the foot. How about the breath? Did it get held, stopped, inhaled or exhaled during the punch?

And, finally, what about the mind? When did the decision get made to throw the punch; and what was going through the mind during and after the punch? The brain made all this happen, was there even awareness of all these elements? If not, could there be? Or at least, be aware of some of them in such a way as to manipulate them to alter the execution.

Now, work with each of these elements, and any more that may be discovered, in any number of combinations; altering their *timings*.

How do those changes affect the overall punch? Do these modifications increase, decrease, or alter the effectiveness of the punch? How about what points and where in the *timing*, if one wanted, would they cause disruption or failure to the maneuver on an opponent? And, could those alterations prevent such a disruption, if one were doing the disruption to them-self?

All points to ponder and explore.

Alignment

Alignment is just putting things in a straight line, right?

Not exactly.

Alignment is putting the proper things in their optimal orientation with each other to create the maximum effect for the intended maneuver - and that arrangement is not always in a straight line.

Probably, a better way to think about alignment is that it is arranging your body to maximize both structure and energy transfer for any specific maneuver.

Quite simply; structure of yourself, to create the ideal result for a maneuver.

> Note: The above statements purposely exclude the use of weapons and any other items that may be used in your **environment**. In other words, it is deliberately only considering your body in this discussion.

So, some readers might be asking:

What exactly is the perfect alignment for each maneuver?

Believe it or not, that is debatable.

Why?

Because different martial art *systems* have different tactics, and therefore the *alignments* can change based upon what their primary *principles*, *considerations*, and *strategies* are; combined with how those components are used to manifest their ultimate aims physically.

> *Note: There is an overlap with the **Principles and Rules**, **Fundamentals**, and **The Human Element** chapters.*

Probably an example is in order:

Compare long-fist kung-fu (northern China) to short-fist kung-fu (southern China).

Do all of their stances, strikes and maneuvers look exactly the same?

Obviously not.

Why?

Because each of them works upon a different set of **strategies**, **principles**, and **considerations**. And, those elements are used to develop the maneuvers used in the martial art.

To highlight one such element:

Long-fist kung-fu is not concerned with confined surroundings, while the short-fist kung-fu is. That **consideration** changes the maneuvers and therefore it's **alignments**.

> *Note: There is an overlap with the **Environment** chapter.*

So, all hope is lost for understanding proper **alignments** then, right?

Absolutely, not.

If one were to break motion down, they would come to the following conclusion:

There are only two (2) types of motion - linear and circular. Knowing that and understanding how the human body creates motion, leads the way to the analysis of **alignment**.

But that statement also generates the following question:

So how does the human body create motion?

Only one major way; joints. And joints only work on circular motion.

All well and good, but this simple fact produces the obvious follow-up question:

So, how does the circular motion of the joints create linear motion?

Any single circular motion cannot create linear motion, only circular motion. But, any two (2) or more circular motions can be combined together to create linear motion.

> Note: In American Kenpo lingo, the central point of the hinge in a joint (or any circular maneuver) is referred to as the pivot point.

So if one stops to think about it, the body structure is just composed of a series of very stiff parts held together with a bunch of hinges. And, therefore, how one positions the stiff parts with the hinges during motion is *alignment*. And, there are a variety of different ways those parts can be positioned. And, the goal is to look at that positioning to determine which best represents the best results for one's specific set of *principles*, *considerations*, and *strategies*.

Two other things to add to this mix are; mass and speed.

First, mass. All parts of our bodies have mass of varying amounts. And, that mass can affect the analysis of one's *alignment*. And, moving that mass creates speed. Those two elements combined together generate power. And, that power is used against one's opponent in some way. But, if that power isn't properly supported (i.e. proper *alignment*), that power can be diminished or rendered in-effective. But, if properly supported, the same power can be accentuated or magnified.

In other words: Proper *alignment* can add to amount of mass that is supporting the maneuver resulting in more power transfer.

> Note: There is an overlap with the **Using Energy** section of **The Human Element** chapter.

> Note: In American Kenpo, there is a famous saying (created by SGM Ed Parker) that goes: *alignment* makes back-up mass possible.

For example:

Imagine a straight punch being executed from a fighting stance.

What mass is being used to transfer the energy into the opponent? Just the mass of the fist? The fist and arm? The fist, arm and body?

If the answer is the last one, then proper *alignment* is needed in order to make sure that the mass of the body is added (i.e. backing up) to the mass of the rest.

If not, then the punch will not be as *effective* as it could be.

So, another way to look at this whole thing is:

More mass = more power: more speed = more power: better alignment = better power transfer. Or, *alignment* makes the other two (2) elements more *effective* and helps with overall power transfer to the opponent.

With the proper understanding of these tools, one can use this knowledge to analyze their maneuvers to work on ensuring proper *alignments* and potentially enhance the *effectiveness* of their movement.

> Note: There is an overlap with the section on **Timing** in this chapter.

One final thought on the matter:

Small adjustments in *alignment* can sometimes have a large positive effect on a maneuver. So, everyone should take the time to look at their current *alignments* and see if maybe a slight drop of an elbow or rotating a hip or foot slightly might enhance the *effectiveness* of the *alignment* and therefore the overall *effectiveness* of the maneuver.

We like to think we are perfect. But often, self-analysis can result in amazing discoveries and improvements.

> Note: What is not being said is that anyone needs to change what they are doing. Just that they take the time to look at the *alignment* of the maneuvers and make sure those *alignments* are proper (for their specific purposes), and as *effective* as they are intended to be.
>
> In other words: It's almost always not one's martial art, rather it's the individual that needs to be adjusted.

Baiting

What if it were possible to have an opponent attack the target of one's choice.

Pretty convenient, right?

That is the idea behind *baiting*. *Baiting* is the active manipulation of the opponent, in an attempt to entice them to attack a specific range of targets or a specific target.

In other words, *baiting* is a relatively simple *strategy* for fooling the opponent into going after a purposely exposed target.

> *Note: There is an overlap with **Preventative and Anticipatory Moves** and **Copying** sections of this chapter.*

So, what's the downside of *baiting*? Why don't we do it all the time?

Because it doesn't always work. Sometimes the opponent sees the *bait* and doesn't fall for it.

And even worst, the opponent may perceive a *bait* and fool one into thinking they are "taking the *bait*" and then turn the *bait* against them. But used effectively, *baiting* can be an exemplary tool for forcing the opponent to the target of one's choosing.

Note/Opinion: One way to look at **baiting** is that it is an attempt to reduce or eliminate required **spontaneity** by manipulating the opponent into doing what one wants, not what the opponent wants.

Note: **Baiting** is a good example of not strictly following short-term **economy** for potential long-term **economy** and **effectiveness**.

Tip: To get the best results from **baiting**, expose only one (1) target area to the opponent. In other words, the **bait** might not work properly if one doesn't purposely cover up all the other potential targets. This may sound obvious, but it is something that can be easily missed.

False Travel

One way in which practitioners think they are being *effective*, but actually aren't, is by falling into the *false travel* trap.

False travel?

A definition is in order:

False travel is when one believes they are executing a weapon with proper travel distance to be *effective*, but in actuality, another part of the body, other than the weapon, is doing most of the travel - thus lulling the practitioner into thinking that the weapon is being *effective*; when it really isn't as *effective* as it could be.

As an example:

Standing in a normal position, with hands at your side, deliver an elbow (with either arm) straight in-front of yourself. If executed as intended, your hand should end up in front of your chest with your elbow pushed forward.

What part of your body moved the most?

Not your elbow; but your hand.

OK, so why is this important to know?

Because we tend to not notice this fact, until it is pointed out. All the motion of the hand, gives the practitioner a sense of a lot of movement, and all that movement must be helping the delivery of the weapon, right?

In short, no.

The majority of the movement (specifically in the hand) is used for aligning the elbow properly; not for improving the travel of the elbow delivery.

> *Opinion: Admittedly, this is probably not the absolute best example, but it is one of the simplest to explain through writing; and it gets the job done.*

Let's take a minute to examine how this situation came about.

First, the elbow is a mid-range weapon. Meaning, there is more to one's arm past the elbow, that can reach further than the elbow. All that extra part of the limb, past one's elbow, needs to be adjusted for both proper formation of the weapon and proper *alignment* of the weapon. So, if the arm is not already positioned properly, it will have to be re-positioned in order to make the elbow *effective*.

In other words, all of that movement may not actually help in the actual delivery of the elbow, but rather just for proper shape and *alignment* of the weapon.

This is where things can get scrambled in one's *mind*. Without stopping to really think about all that movement, one just assumes it was done to help propel the elbow forward. But in fact, most of the movement wasn't.

> *Note: There is a potential overlap with the chapter on* **rationalization**. *But technically, this doesn't really fall into* **rationalization**.

One should take the above example and explanation and use it as a guide into analyzing other movements to ensure that they don't fall into this same conundrum. And, if *false travel* is found, one should find ways to improve the delivery of the weapon to ensure that the weapon is *effective* as anticipated.

*Tip: Elimination of the non-delivery motion isn't required, rather concentrate on the path and travel of the actual weapon. Most of the time this weapon is not the first weapon delivered, but rather one in a series. And as such, a lot of the time, continued motion from prior weapon delivery can be modified to help with reducing non-delivery travel or increasing the path of travel (i.e. **cocking**) for the weapon being scrutinized.*

Copying

There is an interesting quirk that can be exploited by an observant martial artist:

Copying.

This peculiarity of human nature can be described pretty much as what its name says:

Sometimes, opponents will respond to something that is throw or done by repeating exactly the same maneuver.

For example:

If one is sparring with an opponent and throws a back-knuckle; many times, the opponent will respond with throwing a back-knuckle in return.

In other words, they *copy*. Knowing this anomaly, one can use this information to exploit the situation in their favor.

> Note: There is an overlap with the **Patterns** and **Baiting**. sections of this chapter.

One major thing to keep in mind about *copying* is that it isn't completely reliable; a few people (mostly very experienced people) don't *copy* at all; while most will *copy* some of the time, but not always; and a small number (usually an inexperienced person) will *copy* most of the time.

But, *copying* is reliable enough to use as an occasional *strategy*. While this may not be as useful in a purely defensive situation, it does come in handy for sparring and other situations where one has time to observe and/or interact with their opponent. It's fairly easy to probe the opponent to see if they are susceptible to copying.

And finally, like most *strategies* comparable to this one (basically a trick), it pays not to overuse it, because it can be used against the originator, if the opponent gets wise to what is trying to be done.

Now let's look at *copying* from a completely different *perspective*.

When we first learn a martial art, we start out doing exactly what we are told. We spend our time seeking out other, better students or instructors in our studio so that we may *copy* them and become as good as they are. We *copy* what they say and do to better understand and absorb this almost magical material both physically and mentally.

But then, as time passes and we get more experience, skill, and knowledge; we begin to explore our own thoughts on the material and some might even begin to question that material, and even some others may begin to doubt its *effectiveness* or rationale.

And finally, some explore new avenues of thought and experiment with alternative methods of thinking and maneuvering. While some, seek out different instructors or martial arts to help fill their internal void or expand their thinking and skill even further.

Why all this hyperbole and dramatic writing?

Well, essentially this is the history of the martial arts and the point of this book.

We all start out *copying* and eventually either master the material to the point that it isn't really *copying* anymore - it transforms into how and what is natural to do.

But some martial artists explore beyond and are never satisfied with the status quo. It is just in their nature.

It is said that the best form of flattery is imitation; another word for *copying*.

Masters don't *copy*, they assimilate and make it their own.

Why?

Because, they understand the structure, composition and fundamentals of the information being presented. They can take it apart and put it back together in a form of their choosing. Or, they can meld it so well with their own way, it is no longer a *copy* - it is theirs. Or, even in some cases, information and maneuvers are analyzed and rejected as not fitting with their specific vision of the martial arts.

> *Opinion: The problem with* **systems** *(any system - not just the martial arts) is that innovation and new thinking is discouraged and often rejected out of hand, at first, until the new train of thought and way is accepted by the masses of the* **system***. And, then the cycle starts again.*

> *Opinion: Just because one changes things doesn't mean what they are doing is unique, correct, or even good. One of the biggest problems with humans is that they often are convinced that they (and primarily they) are right and brilliant (and amazing). If one is going to change things; they must first make sure they FULLY understand what it is they are changing.*
>
> *In other words, don't be a rebel for being a rebel's sake. Instead, first become a master and then innovate.*

Final Thoughts

Learning to be "the best you can be", at least in this context, sounds easy and very straight forward. Don't be fooled, it can very difficult to recognize and harder to achieve.

One of the major things to look out for is self-delusion. It is very easy to fall into the trap of thinking one is better, more *efficient* and more *effective* than they actually are.

In other words, don't fool yourself - instead be your own worst critic. Always strive to find and eliminate waste in not only obvious and mundane ways, but try to think outside the box every once in a while.

> Note: There is an overlap with the **Perspective** and **Rationalization** chapters.

One really helpful exercise to locate faults and improve one's self is through video. Every so often, one should video themself, and take a good long look at what they are doing and make sure what is on the video is what is anticipated. If there are any discrepancies, there is work to do. And (this should go without saying), one should be brutally honest with them-self.

Once one has gotten through all that, they should then look at them-self from the standpoint of the opponent and how that person could take advantage of what is seen. If one thinks that they could beat them-self in combat, again there's work to do.

Finally, one should look at the video from different angles. For instance, watch it upside down, backwards, or with only peripheral vision. What's wrong? What's right? What can be improved or corrected?

> *Note: Learning to recognize inefficient and/or ineffective motion is only half the battle. Sometimes one will say to them-self:*
>
> *I know something is wrong, but I can't put my finger on what, or how I would go about fixing it.*
>
> *This is a very common issue that will lessen over time and practice.*
>
> *There are generally two immediate and practical solutions to this problem:*
>
> *1) either one should continue to work the problem it is solved or*
>
> *2) help should be elicited from someone else to see what they see and say.*
>
> *Sometimes someone else will notice the problem and solution, or start one down a path that progresses them into solve the problem on their own.*

And finally, one should learn to be observant of others - other martial arts, sports, exercise, and any other form of movement. Learn to tell the difference between someone who is **effective** and **efficient** with their movements from one who is not. And then, learn what could be done to improve their own motion.

One should go over in their **mind** how they would interact with those individuals, given the chance, on improvements and adjustments to their movements.

In short, become a martial arts **kinesiologist** - someone who studies the mechanics of body movements as they relate to martial arts.

Note: There is an overlap with the **Body/Anatomy and Kinesiology** section of **The Human Element** chapter.

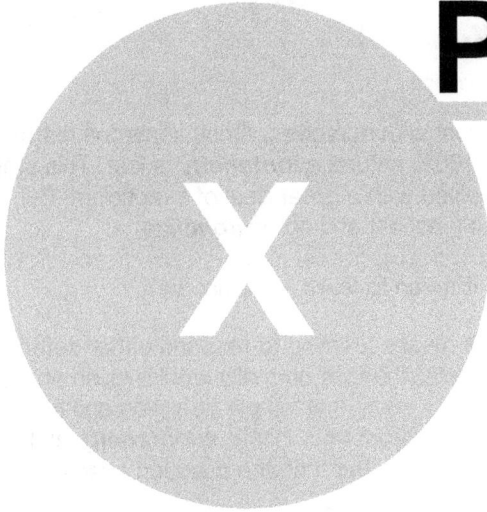

Part

X

Spontenaity

Overview

Let's be honest with ourselves. Once someone learns any martial art, 100% natural *spontaneity* is lost. This statement may be received with a great deal of skepticism. But again, let's be completely honest and not *rationalize*.

What does it mean to learn a martial art?

At its core, it means learning to respond either defensively or offensively better than we normally would; given an aggressive situation. And as such, that simple definition and its implementation disrupts our innate *spontaneity* and replaces it with something else. But then the question arises:

Is that a bad thing or a good thing?

For the most part, that is a good thing. One learns to get rid of the ineffective and inefficient and replace it with something more *efficient* and *effective*. All good.

> Note: There is an overlap with the **Rationalization** and **Economy, Efficiency, and Effectiveness** chapters.

Now for the bad part.

Because we are not being completely and naturally *spontaneous*, but rather have replaced our normal responses with a martial art *system*; we can quickly fall into the *If This Then That pattern*.

In short, this means one can become predictable and repetitious. One will respond with what they were taught, automatically. And, if someone knows or perceives this fact, they can also possibly exploit it.

> *Note: There is an overlap with the sections **If This Then That** and **Reflex vs Thought** in this chapter.*

For example:

Probably every reader has been in the situation where they saw a new instructor, seminar, or instructional situation and said to themselves:

Wow, that (those) guy(s) look(s) pretty cool and the stuff he (they) is (are) doing looks really good!

But, after continuing to watch for a while, they then say to themself:

Hmm, he (they) keep doing the same stuff over and over again.

And, amazingly enough, it's not as magical as when it was first observed. It still may be cool, but the initial luster has faded. The question is:

Why?

Because the motion has now become a recognizable and understandable *pattern*. And *patterns* can be predicted and exploited.

> *Note: there is an overlap with the section **Patterns** in the chapter **Economy, Efficiency, and Effectiveness**.*

In other words, if one replaces their natural *spontaneity* with a martial art *system*, someone else with the proper knowledge and training may be able to potentially predict what a given response might be, provided with a specific input. And, that could be a problem.

Maybe not against an untrained individual, but very possibly against another practitioner trained in the same art or maybe just a very astute and well trained practitioner with a knowledge of that specific *system*.

Opinion: Admittedly, this specific situation is not common, but should definitely be acknowledged, considered, and examined.

As stated in other parts of this book, there are martial arts that specifically target recognizable maneuvers and take advantage of their specific, known characteristics; such as balance, **timing**, and positioning. This should not be ignored or overlooked.

If This Then That

If this then that is fundamentally how any martial art is formulated. It basically is the following logic:

If you do this, then I'll do that.

Simple enough. But, like all processes or **strategies**, there is a downside.

In this case, at its core, *if this then that* is a **pattern**. And like all **patterns**, it can be exploited.

But all hope is not lost. If one stops to think about it for a minute, they will come to the understanding that any single *if this* scenario can have a multitude of *then that* responses.

So, how is that helpful?

Think about it from this standpoint:

If someone had ten (10) *then that* responses to a given *if this* scenario; how is that, from a practical and real-world standpoint, much different from **spontaneity**? How could the other person guess which *then that* was going to be executed?

In other words, at some point, multiple *then that's* become almost indistinguishable from **spontaneity**, from the **perspective** of the receiver of the response.

> Note: In American Kenpo lingo, the above scenario can also be referred to as position recognition.

From the above statements the following question arises:

How many *then that's* does one need for a specific *if then*?

Probably, the bare minimum is two (2) responses. A more reasonable number should be between three (3) and (5) responses. But obviously, the more *then that's* one has for a given *if this* the closer to *spontaneity* one approaches; and therefore, the harder to predict which *then that* will be chosen and countered.

And to add more to the above discussion, the more diverse the *then that's* are the better the chance that any multiple *then that's* can be foiled with the same counter measure.

In other words, the *then that's* should be as wildly different and non-similar as possible to prevent the opponent from stopping multiple *then that's* with the same counter response.

> *Note: The reader should take the above statement from a personal **perspective** and use it against the opponent.*
>
> *In other words, don't forget that you can do the same to your opponent - i.e. come up with a counter-measure that can be used against the opponent's **then that** maneuver(s).*
>
> *And, the most effective optimal counter-measure is the one that can be used against any and all of your opponent's **then that** maneuvers.*

There is still one major downside to consider when having many *then that* responses to a given *if this* scenario:

Which *then that* am I going to use?

If one has too many *then that* responses, choosing which one may slow their response time to the *if then*, and as such the *efficiency* of their response time may suffer. That is why most practitioners will have a default or favorite one or two *then that* responses.

And with that, the struggle between *spontaneity*, *patterns* (i.e. predictability), and *efficiency* continues.

Note: The technical name for the above paragraph is referred to as the Hick-Hyman law. This law basically states that the decision time (and therefore a slower response time) of an individual increase with the number of potential options to consider and ultimately choose.

Reflex vs Thought

Why do we train?

The simple answer is to get better. But what does that really mean?

It can mean we become more comfortable with both the physical and mental aspects of what we are training in.

It also means that we become more *economical*, *efficient* and *effective* in both our motion and *thought*.

And, what happens if we continue to train? Do we get to a point where we are as optimal as we can get? And, what about the *mental* aspect of that training? Can we get to a point where our mind just reacts without much forethought? Or, do we always need to think about everything first?

All really interesting questions to ponder.

> Note: There is an overlap with the chapter on **Economy, Efficiency, and Effectiveness**.

But first, THE most important thing to understand is that:

You will react like you train.

If one trains ineffectively, they will react ineffectively. If one trains without full effort, they will react without full effort. Without question, and without exception, everyone WILL become the product of their training.

In short, one should NEVER *rationalize* about their training and believe they are above this simple, inescapable principle! Because if they do, they will become a (potentially unknowing) subject of it.

> Note: There is an overlap with the chapter on
> **Rationalization**.

> Opinion: Everyone believes that their training is deadly,
> **effective**, **efficient**, optimal, awesome, etc... Everyone
> should take the time to stop and objectively analyze their
> training.
>
> Most people just train the way they were taught, without
> truly stopping and looking at the actual mechanics and
> results of that training.
>
> Everyone should do them-self a favor, at least once
> throughout their martial arts career, they should step
> back and analyze their training from a dispassionate and
> critical **perspective**. And adjust accordingly.

Okay, okay, all very interesting, but what does this have to do
with the title of this section?

In short, one's training will become their *reflexive* reaction to
surprise situations. If one is taken unaware, their natural
reaction will be their training.

To answer one of the questions above:

Repetitive training eventually becomes *reflexive* and requires
little to no *thought* on the practitioner's part.

And, to change a *reflexive* reaction takes a lot of time and
work. So, proper training is essential.

Anecdote/Opinion: The martial arts are replete with stories of individuals who have trained for years a specific way or in a specific art, but then decided to change their training somewhere along the line. Practically everyone comments about how hard it was and how long it took to undo the engrained effects from their original training.

Another way to look at this is:

We are training to not only improve physically, but also to allow our *mind* to react more *reflexively*, without allowing *thoughts* to get in the way, thus slowing the whole process down.

The big trick is to train properly and repetitively, such that the *mind* accepts the maneuvers and moves them from only conscious *thought* into muscle and *reflexive* memory. So that when the time and situation presents itself, the reaction will stem from a *reflexive* and relatively *spontaneous* manner, rather than with a pensive and/or undisciplined one.

*Note: There is an overlap with the **Patterns** section in the **Economy, Efficiency, and Effectiveness** chapter.*

Note: A very good book that spends a lot of time and detail about this subject and how it relates to stressful situations is "On Combat" by Lt. Col. Dave Grossman. He has a second book that is also highly recommended reading - "On Killing."

Final Thoughts

This chapter started out basically stating that once an individual start training in the martial arts, natural *spontaneity* is lost. But, is it really? If it is replaced with something just as *efficient* in time and more *effective* in result, does it matter?

If summed up, the major unwritten theme within this whole chapter is:

Learning how to get out of your own mind and letting your body respond 'naturally' with your martial art, just better than before you started training.

> Note: There is an overlap with the **Economy, Efficiency, and Effectiveness** chapter.

The above statement is really one of our major goals for starting to learn martial arts in the first place.

The tough part of all this discussion is our *mind*, not our body.

Letting our training seep into our subconscious *mind* to the point that it becomes our new 'natural' response. Getting to the point where we no longer need to think about specific defenses or responses to a given offensive situation.

That is why there is repetition - and lots of it. Many people believe it is to get better physically. They are partially right, but that is only half the battle. The other half is teaching our *mind* that what we are doing is good in an attempt to make it our default response. We will respond to a threat, but how?

In other words, we all train in an effort to make us better without thinking about it, when the time comes.

> Note: There is an overlap with **The Human Element** chapter.

Part

XI

Principles and Rules

Overview

Everyone has beliefs. It's human nature. Be it religion, politics, or how to live your life; beliefs permeate our lives - both ours and others. Another thing about human nature is that we like to *organize* things. And when we combine those two (2) traits about a specific subject, what was once just a random set of convictions, gets transformed into a belief system.

In other words, belief systems are just a structured set of beliefs around a specific subject.

All well and good, but this chapter is on *principles and rules*. What do belief systems have to do with *principles and rules* and of the martial arts?

Because *principles* are the codified expression of a belief. And, a *rule* is the statement of boundaries or expression of a *principle*.

In other words, one starts with beliefs, from those beliefs a *principle* or set of *principles* are formed, and from those *principles* a set of *rules* emerge to add structure and limits to the active demonstration of those *principles*.

So, these statements can lead to the following potential conclusion:

Then a martial arts system is just a set of beliefs, expressed in its *principles and rules*.

And that conclusion would be correct.

If one stops to think about it, all martial arts systems can be broken down into an understanding of how self-defense "should" be executed - from their point of view (a.k.a. belief system).

Note: There is an overlap with the **Nuance** section in the **Fundamentals** chapter.

Another way to look at it:

So, we want to create our own martial arts *system*. How do we do it?

In practical terms, one would inherently start by laying out their ideas about their beliefs in regards to self-defense.

In other words, what is this new marital art supposed to accomplish and what concepts are going to be expressed - both physically and mentally?

Then, every element and action of this new martial art would work towards achieving that vision. And finally, with each new piece, the do and do nots of this marital art will emerge. Most of this could happen with or without one openly naming or writing all this stuff down. It will all just be the natural expression of the new *system*.

For example, and exercise:

Let's take Tai Chi Chuan. Can we spell out the fundamental beliefs of this *system*? One may not get them all, but everyone reading would probably get at least one:

Practice everything very slowly and precisely.

It's just that clear and obvious that this is a major hallmark of the *system*. Simple, obvious, and never compromised.

Then, with that determination, rules can be formulated, like:

Move as slow as you need to, to do everything very exacting. Or, don't rush through the form. Take your time.

Note: The above example could have been for any martial art. Tai Chi Cuan was chosen because most people have a basic exposure to it and because it's very distinctive style.

Defining Terms

It is always important to clarify exactly what we are talking about. Therefore, like other places in this book, let's start with specific definitions:

Principle

1. A fundamental truth, proposition or building block that serves as a foundation for a system.

2. A base contractual or conventional element of a system.

Rule

1. A prescribed guide for conduct or action.

2. An accepted procedure, custom or habit.

3. A regulation or limitation of behavior within a particular activity or sphere.

In a simplistic way, the *principles* of a martial art can be thought of as the martial art's mission statement. It lays out what everyone in the *system* should know and understand as the basis of that *system*. And, those tenants should never be violated.

Where *rules* are basically the code of conduct of the martial art. They are things that should not be broken, but under certain circumstances can be.

Another way to look at these definitions is from a hierarchical standpoint. *Principles* are at the top and are fundamental; never defied; and rarely, if ever changed. They are the expression of core beliefs.

In other words, they are the ultimate aims and goals of the *system*.

For instance, if a martial art has as a *principle*:

One will never back up.

Then nowhere in the expression of the *system* will anyone back up - ever. It just would not be done. But, if someone backed up somewhere in execution, it would be in conflict with the *principle*.

Given that situation, only a number of things could occur:

First, the practitioner would not be doing the martial art correctly (from the standpoint of the *system* and its *principles*), and would need to change what they are doing to comply with the stated *principle*.

Or second, the *principle(s)* is(are) not understood or expressed correctly and would therefore need to be updated or altered. One possible modification to the *principle* could be:

Backing up is only done as a last resort.

Underneath *principles* in the hierarchy would be *rule*.

A *rule* should be thought of as an expression of the *principles* of the *system*. So, if a *principle* of a martial art was:

Always try to create a stable stance.

Then there would be *rules* around how to do this. For example:

Always punch or block after getting into a stance.

But, there might be situations where one *rule* takes precedent over another *rule*. In such a case, one may need to break one *rule* to obey another. And that is OK.

Adding to the above example: there may be another rule that says:

Never let your opponent touch you.

And given a very specific scenario in which the *rules* are in conflict; which *rule* would be considered more important - the stable stance or not being touched?

The answer lies in the individual and their interpretation of the *rules* and *principles*.

> *Note: There is an overlap with the **Consideration Priority** section of this chapter.*

Further Exploration

Another example of ***principles and rules*** in action:

In boxing, why is it illegal to punch below the belt?

Because one of the founding beliefs of the sport is that it is gentlemanly. And, therefore the derived principle is:

One should always act like a gentleman in the ring.

That ***principle*** then expresses itself as the ***rule***:

fighters cannot punch below the belt.

Why?

Because it is not gentlemanly.

The important thing to take-away from this is that the ***principle*** is the stated belief and the ***rule*** obeys and expresses that belief.

Principles are fairly obvious, and once set, are never (or rarely) changed. They are intended to be clearly defined expressions of the beliefs of the ***system***. Truths that should not be defied.

But ***rules*** can get a little trickier. One reason is because ***rules*** can be looked at from two (2) points of view.

A ***rule*** can be thought of as an expression of the ***principles*** of a ***system***. This is how it is generally represented by definitions #1 and #2 and as we have discussed it up to now. It is more like a guide and is designed to aid in proper action. Pretty straight forward and innocent.

In other words, tell me what I'm supposed to do and not do to obey my ***system***. We can call these types of ***rules***, ***rules*** of expression.

But then there is definition #3 - limiting behavior.

Rules that explicitly limit what can and cannot be done. We can refer to these as limiter *rules*. These are the ones we need to look out for and be careful of. Because they are *rules* of penalty and discipline.

At first glance, the definitions may sound pretty much the same. And on the surface, they appear that way. But, let's look at what is being said a little more closely.

Expression *rules* can be thought of as *rules*, that if broken, will only pose a risk from and by the opponent(s).

In other words, one breaks them at the risk of being beaten by the opponent.

But breaking a limiter *rule*, on the other hand, is recognized and punished by a third party - not the opponent(s).

In other words, if one breaks a limiter *rule* then an official or mediator will be the one that makes the practitioner pay the penalty for breaking it. The opponent may recognize the breaking of the *rule*, but unless they are the official or mediator, there is really nothing they can do about it.

A reasonably good, but not entirely on point, example:

The U.F.C. started out as a no-holds-barred fighting challenge between different martial arts. Compare that with current M.M.A.

They are kind of the same thing, but what happened?

Rules! Lots of them.

Whether this is good or bad is not the point. But there is no denying that the original U.F.C. bares only a scant resemblance to what it transformed into.

In fact, M.M.A. is now mostly considered its own *system*. And as such, follows it's own *principles and rules*; and they are not the same as the original U.F.C.

In the first situation, most of the *rules* where expression *rules*; *rules* expressed by the opponents as it pertained to their discipline, not by the officials. Arguably, that is no longer the case.

Another way to look at limiter *rules* is:

Limiter *rules*, if not used properly, can turn a martial art into a sport.

Wait, what? Sharp left turn! You lost me!

OK, Look at it from this point of view:

If this new martial art has a bunch of limiter *rules*, like:

No poking the eye. No striking to the groin. No purposely break anything on the opponent.

At what point do the above *rules* become so limiting of behavior that it loses the essence of a true martial art and moves into the realm of a sport?

Positive vs Negative Rules

Now *rules* looked at from a completely different angle.

There are basically two (2) types of *rules*: positive *rules* and negative *rules*.

In other words, *rules* that say what one should do and *rules* that say what one shouldn't do.

An example of a positive *rule*:

Always get into a good stance.

An example of a negative *rule*:

Never attack or defend without first being in a good stance.

They both pretty much say the same thing, but do it from the *opposite* standpoint.

At this point, the following questions may arise:

Is there really a difference? Which is better? Does it matter?

> Note: There is an overlap here with the **Opposite and Reverses** and **Perspective** chapters.

In a general sense, it doesn't really matter which way a rule is stated, but there are subtle psychological differences and tendencies.

Positive *rules* tend to spell out correct conduct. As such, they are less likely to veer a martial art into limits and more likely to keep it on course - by guiding.

Why?

Because positive incentives tend to more directly illustrate the underlying *principle(s)*. Not that negative *rules* can't; just that positive *rules* tend to do it more naturally and gently. Where negative *rules* tend to express more of an immediacy, urgency, or penalty.

> *Opinion: To express positive **rules**, one should use the word "always." To express negative **rules**, one should rely upon the word "never."*

> *Opinion: Keep in mind that **rules** can be broken. So, one should remember that **rules** are designed to be obeyed 99% of the time. There are almost always exceptions to the **rules**.*

In other words, don't stop using negative *rules*; just try to remember that positive *rules* have a tendency to outdo negative *rules* in expressing *principles* without as much potential for negative consequences.

But on the other hand, if that is exactly what response one is trying to prompt, a negative *rule* can be the better choice.

One final observation:

As implied above, negative *rules* also tend to be better limiter *rules*. Positive *rules* tend to be better expression *rules*. This is not always the case, but a majority of the time it is.

An example of a positive limiter *rule*:

One must always kick below the head.

But, expressed as a negative *rule*:

Never kick to the head.

Usually, the example limiter *rule* would be expressed as a negative *rule*; but as one can see, it can also be expressed positively.

*Note: In reading the **opposite and reverse** chapter, some readers may have noticed that the example of the Paxial arts was given. Notice how it's **principles and rules** were so directly in opposition to most of the general martial arts **principles and rules** that even the name was changed away from "martial art." Not a sport or martial art - a Paxial art.*

Consideration Priority

One of the most used words in this book is *consider*. Let's face it, in martial arts there are a lot of things to *consider*. Elements in this book, like: *environment*; *principles and rules*; *perspective*; and *effectiveness*. But there are many others that are not even explicitly called out, like; motivation, size, strength, and number of opponents; for starters. All of these get thrown into the hopper of one's *mind* at some point during their advancement through their art.

> Note: There is an overlap with **The Human Element** chapter.

At this point, this very important question arises:

How is a practitioner supposed to organize and make sense of all this stuff in a defensive situation quickly and *effectively*?

For the most part, the martial art that they train in should resolve the majority of this issue.

In other words, the *principles and rules* along with the *strategies* of the martial art should give definite *priorities* as to what to *consider* and when. Then, continued training in that martial art is designed to help tune those responses into *reflex*.

If one stops to think about what learning a martial art truly is, from one *perspective*, it's about learning a set of beliefs about self-defense and then learning how to apply those beliefs in real-world situations.

> *Opinion: One thing that is almost always overlooked or not taken into* **consideration** *enough is the use of video (primarily cell phone video). This is mostly because it is such a new technology and all of the classical (and even modern arts) were created prior to this technology being pervasive.*
>
> *One should automatically assume there is a video being taken of the situation and act accordingly.*

So, from the above statement, the only time a practitioner should really need to think about and **consider** things (from a self-defense **perspective**) is when there is a conflict or overlap in the **principles** or **rules** of the system. The less overlap, the less decision making, and therefore, the quicker the response time.

In other words, it is not the responsibility of the practitioner to try and minimize this conflict or overlap, it is the sole responsibility of the **system**.

> *Note: There is an overlap with the chapter on* **Spontaneity***.*

Therefore, if a practitioner of an art were to analyze a given response in a training and/or combat environment, they should be able to extrapolate the **rules** and **principles** that are applied to the response. And those **principles and rules** should directly correlate back to and be totally congruent with their **system**.

In other words, what a practitioner is taught to do in a self-defense situation should be in total harmony with the **principles and rules** of their art. And if any practitioner wanted to, they should be able to call out what **principles and rules** were applied during the execution of the specified response.

So, in summary, there are a lot of things for a practitioner to **consider**. But it is primarily the job of the **system** to resolve those **considerations** and **prioritize** them for the practitioner.

That way, the practitioner can concentrate their efforts on learning the *system* with a minimized set of *considerations*; and therefore, faster responses.

> *Opinion: Teaching what and how a* ***system*** *prioritizes* ***considerations*** *ultimately falls on the responsibility of the instructor. This requires a competent instructor to become keenly aware of this knowledge in order to properly pass it on it to students.*
>
> But as eluded to above, the adept practitioner might also be able to extract the same information from their training, given inadequate and correct information about their *system*. But they shouldn't need to.

Style vs System

Believe it or not, the following can be a fairly common discussion starter (paraphrased) among advanced practitioners:

OK, so what happens if I don't fully believe and obey all of the *rules* and actions of my martial art? I modified some stuff to make it fit myself. Does that mean I have my own *system*?

In general, no. In concise terms, what is being described is a *style* change, not a *system* change.

So, what's the difference?

The way to think about *style* is that it is one's personal manner of expressing a *system*.

To come at it from another point of view:

Where the underlying *principles* of the *system* changed?

If not, then we are still within the same *system*. One is just expressing the same *system* with their own "flair" or "style."

For example:

Take the martial art Goju-ryu. There are distinct *styles* of Goju-ryu, such as; Nisei, Urban, Eibu Kan, and Ichikawa-ha to name a few. None of these *styles* consider themselves a different *system*, just an expression of the parent martial art, Goju-ryu.

But then the following question arises:

When do the accumulation of changes get to the point where a new *system* is created?

And, that is where *principles* come into play. If the accumulating alterations begin to affect the underlying *principles* of the *system*, then it becomes arguable about the *system* changing, and discussions about being considered a new *system* may be appropriate.

Up to that point, though, there are just *stylistic* changes.

> *Opinion: Hobbling together a bunch of stuff from a bunch of different **systems** does not create a new **system**.*
>
> *Rather, it's usually just what it sounds like; a stitching together of in-cohesive set of potentially conflicting **principles**.*
>
> *Creating a **system** takes thought, understanding, intelligence, planning, training, patience, and a lot of skill.*
>
> *Studying a bunch of systems and cherry picking what one likes does not create a **system** - it most often it creates an incomprehensible mess held together by a lone individual or very small group.*

Final Thoughts

It is debatable that of all the topics explored in this book, *principles and rules* are probably the hardest to understand as being directly tied to practicality in the martial arts.

In other words, it's easy for someone to say:

This as just a bunch of technical mumbo jumbo.

But, if one takes the time to pause and think about what *principles and rules* actually are, they cannot be avoided or completely overlooked.

At some point in one's training, practice, or thinking; a *rule* or *principle* about their actions will become self-evident.

Otherwise, what is one really learning?

So, it's this chapter's assertion that it's better to have a thorough understanding of these concepts, and that *principles and rules* be explained and exposed as the helpful tools they correctly are.

Yes, they are technical in nature, and sometimes boring. But they are undeniably useful mechanisms to aid in determining correctness and boundaries on action and thought.

Give them a chance. Add them to your thinking and practice. You never know, you might just get to like them and use them. You can't avoid them. Even if you try.

Comment: The above comments are deliberately tongue-in-cheek. A lot of martial artists like the physicality of the martial arts and only sometimes tolerate the cerebral stuff. This is just a fun and humorous poke at that mindset; combined with a reminder to, hopefully, not forget that the boring stuff can also be important. Even if we don't normally think about it very often.

Part

XII

Nuance

Overview

How can someone spend literally their entire life learning a martial art? Once we learn to stand, block and/or strike isn't that all? Why put so much time and effort into something that can be construed as so repetitive?

To any serious practitioner of the martial arts, these questions may seem somewhat absurd. But taken at face value, how would these questions be answered?

Probably, most practitioners would say something like:

it's an art. That's how.

And, they would be right. But, what does that answer really mean? In one word - *nuance*.

Just like any other form of art, martial art is replete with *nuance*.

Not only is *nuance* the subtle and no-so-subtle differences in how different martial art *systems* approach conflict. But more specifically it is the small details contained within the various drills, maneuvers, *strategies*, and concepts that compose a particular martial art.

It is the scrutiny, specificity, *categorization*, and analysis of thought and movement.

It is the engine to the potentially harmonious alignment of body and mind toward a singular result.

It is the quest for perfect representation of *principles*, concepts, and physical motion.

It is the never-ending goal toward not only success, but victory with skill and efficacy.

In other words, it's an art. And, to excel at any art it requires time, patience, and dedication.

The martial arts are no different.

> *Note: There is potential overlap with the **Principles and Rules** chapter.*

Two (2) very interesting aspects about **nuance** as it relates to the martial arts are:

That it is everywhere and it is hidden in plain sight. **Nuance** can be found in the simplest of acts, such as a stance, a block, or a punch.

And, if viewed from an uninitiated eye, goes completely unnoticed. Not until the **nuance** is exposed does the uninitiated person understand and can appreciate the amount of time, effort, and skill that goes into the mastery of seemingly effortless acts.

And, since **nuance** permeates just about everything martial artists do, it is not surprising at all that it can take a lifetime or more to refine one's self to the point that the initiated eye can state that the intended **nuance** has been expressed effectively and sufficiently.

> *Opinion: The Japanese tea ceremony is a prime example of **nuance** at some of its finest.*

> *Note: In many respects, there is a potentially large overlap between **nuance** and Zen. Some may go so far as to say they are fairly close to the same thing.*

Physical

So, what causes this *nuance*?

When one thinks of *nuance*, one usually is thinking about physical *nuance* - *nuance* of motion and movement. And from this *perspective*, the major cause is the number of physical variables that go into even the simplest of movements and how a specific art interprets the minor variances as being useful or not.

> Note: There is an overlap with the **Principles and Rules** chapter.

For example:

How long does it take a child to learn to walk?

It varies, but very rarely does a child just stand up and start walking. It can take days, weeks, or months. But now we can do it without even thinking about it. And, we can point out people that walk "askew or different."

Why?

Because walking is a physically complicated action. There is great deal of balance and muscular coordination required to successfully walk: and it takes time to conquer the specifics.

But, simultaneously as we have overcome the physical complications of the act we also built a mental picture of what correct walking is in our *mind*. And, people who have a variance in our standard interpretation of how to walk well, can be spotted very quickly.

This is very similar to how it works in the martial arts.

Note: There is an overlap with the chapter on **Economy, Efficiency, and Effectiveness**.

As one learns a martial art, they are taught roughly correct motion, at first. Then as the practitioner's motion improves, more layers of **nuance** are added in an effort to more approximate the "perfect" intended motion. Elements such as:

Body alignment, sequence of engaging body parts, **timing** of muscle engagement, weight shifting, energy output, and perceived **intent** all add to the **nuance** that the instructor sees in their **mind's** eye.

Any minute variance can easily be spotted by a highly trained individual. And, all of this is done without an opponent. And, as such this method of **nuance** layering continues again and again with more variables and corrections.

So, when does this perfecting process end?

As implied throughout this entire chapter; in all reality, never.

There will always be potential improvements, discoveries, and/or physical changes that one has to adapt to throughout one's life. And, a real **master** never feels as if they have fully perfected these motions - ever. They continually feel that there is always a need for self-improvement.

*Note: Another way to think about the above paragraph is that an instructor does not teach a white belt the same **nuance** as a black belt, they teach them with white belt expectations.*

*When the student achieves black belt, the instructor no longer teaches the student the **nuance** of a white belt, they teach them with black belt **nuance** and expectations.*

*And finally, as a **master**, the practitioner continues to teach them-self with ever increasing expectations and perfection of **nuance**.*

*Opinion: A true **grand master** reaches a **physical** or **mental** level of **nuance** perfection that even the highly initiated practitioner is awed with the almost magical qualities that the **grand master** has achieved - i.e. the sheer and almost complete mastery of the art.*

Mental

As mentioned earlier, a trained eye can distinguish **nuance** in a physical maneuver. But then the following question arises:

How can one really know what another individual is thinking or understanding?

And, that is the problem with mental **nuance**.

Just because an instructor makes a statement, doesn't mean the practitioner(s) fully understand(s) what was said. Each individual has their own capacity, abilities, and experiences that may influence how they interpret the spoken word.

For example:

Sometimes a statement can be made numerous times by one individual without full mental penetration by another. The practitioner understands what is being said, but it doesn't "sink in." But if a different individual says the same thing, only in a slightly different manner (or maybe even changing a single word), the practitioner finally "gets it."

> Note: Another way to accomplish the same output as the example is to completely re-phrased the statements, coming to the same end-point from a totally different **perspective** - usually one that the individual can relate to. This can often add the "missing element" that prevents the individual from comprehending the meaning and **intent** of the statements.

But, to be fair, the above discourse still doesn't really answer the original question. The real answer to the question is:

There is no definitive way to know for absolute certainty what another person is really thinking and understanding.

But, one of the best means to "view" understanding and mental *nuance* is through teaching. And by teaching, it is meant that the practitioner teaches to another person. And during that instruction, the new "student" is directed to ask the "instructor" questions about what they are saying and trying to teach. Through that directed back-and-forth the *nuance* of the thoughts can be extracted, analyzed and corrected as needed.

> *Opinion: One very effective method is that the instructor pretends to be a smart student that asks very probing questions about what is being taught.*

The major problem with the above approach is that it doesn't scale very well.

In other words, this approach works well in low number settings, but is almost impossible to be entirely *effective* with large numbers. That is why many instructors reserve this type of training to select students and "instructors-in-training."

There is however a scaled-down approach that can be relatively effective and is more commonly used as a replacement (or extension) to the previous method. And, almost everyone knows this one:

The question and answer scenario.

This is where the instructor asks the practitioner(s) questions that are to be answered. This is probably the most effective method of eliciting understood information from individuals in a large number situation.

> *Note / Opinion: There is a very major problem that everyone should be aware of with question-and-answer of one's own students (and potentially other students of the same art). It can be coined the "parrot syndrome."*
>
> *This is where the student(s) answer(s) the question with (almost) exactly the same words that they were taught in the first place. This gives the instructor the illusion that the practitioner understood the lesson; when, in fact, they just spouted the words they were taught back, without any "real" understanding of the **nuance** of the instruction.*
>
> *Be very aware of this problem. As the instructor, one may be very proud of their pupil quoting the answer "properly" back to them. But, always keep in mind that those words may have no real or deep "meaning" to the student.*
>
> *The quickest way to uncover the "parrot syndrome" is to ask follow-up and more probing questions about what the answer meant.*

All-in-all, **mental nuance** is just as difficult a component to pass on as **physical nuance**. And, without the properly developed skills to impart information to another **effectively**, large elements of an art can be quickly diminished over the course of just a few generations.

Opinion: If one is serious about becoming an instructor and teaching their art to others, they should also take the time to learn how to teach not only the physical elements of the art, but also the mental elements of the art.

Teaching is a skill unto itself. It should not be overlooked as such.

Opinion: A true **grand master** does not put self-limits on conceptual exploration and/or **mental nuance**. They should be open to exploring any avenue of thought in an effort to not only continue their art, but also expand it within its defined **principles**.

Final Thoughts

So, with all this talk about *nuance* one of the "elephant in the room" sentiments that arise is:

What about the student that just wants to learn to defend them-self? Where does *nuance* fit with them?

It must be understood that not everyone that learns a martial art wants to become an instructor of that art. Instead, their motivation may be short-term - learning enough to become effective and gain the confidence that they may be lacking.

With this comes the question that each instructor must ask them-self:

How much *nuance* am I going to try to teach this student?

And, that answer can only be answered by the instructor. Any answer that is given in this book would just be a blatant (and probably not accurate) opinion.

> *Opinion: We as martial artists often assume that everyone wants to be a martial artist.*
>
> *And that is just false.*
>
> *Everyone has different goals that they want to achieve from their involvement in the martial arts.*
>
> *We must understand that and try not to "pigeon hole" everyone into our personal motivations. As a business and as a person, this can be extremely difficult to achieve and deal with on a day-to-day basis.*

One thing to keep in mind, though, is that often times a new practitioner's motivations change over time. It is not uncommon for a person that just wants to learn to defend them-self to get caught up in the skill that they are learning and want to progress further than they originally imagined. And, sometimes the reverse is true.

We instructors, as keepers of our art, must be keenly aware of this fact and learn to adapt accordingly to both situations.

> *Note: There is a potential overlap with* **Students** *section in the* **Fundamentals** *chapter.*

Part

XIII

Organization, Classification, and Categorization

Overview

So, you have some really good ideas about the martial arts. Good for you. No really, good for you.

But, what does one do with them?

Without a doubt the first thing one must do is not forget them.

Sounds ludicrous, but most good ideas will be forgotten if not preserved somehow - and quickly.

Also, extremely important is that one must make sure that these good ideas are preserved in a state, and with enough detail and pertinent context, that they may be accurate reminders of the original thought. Especially after a long period of time. This is a critical fact, and can't be understated.

If one doesn't do all this, then recreating these ideas in the future may be extremely difficult or impossible. There is a very real possibility that one may be totally lost when reading the saved information after an extended period of time. Or, maybe only able to partially recall the saved thought.

This is not preposterous, but a fact. Rest assured, from experience and anecdotal information from reliable sources, it isn't.

> *Note/Opinion: Recalling saved facts, rules, or statements is far easier than recalling whole, complex thoughts or not fully flushed out theories. Getting one's head back into the same mindset from reading may require a good deal of context. This context may be facts, situational, or whatever works for the individual.*
>
> *In short, there is no real set process that works for everyone.*

It doesn't really matter how one records their thoughts. Some like old school paper notes. Some like audio or video recordings, some like computer programs; some use a combination.

The specifics don't matter, just these two (2) particulars:

The thoughts have to be readily retrievable when needed; and the notes must be memorable.

OK, so you now have a bunch of saved thoughts on the martial arts. Again, good for you.

And again, what does one do with them?

Believe it or not, martial arts is not unlike many of the sciences and philosophies that we as humans think about and study.

And, how do others deal with a bunch of information on a specific subject?

They **organize**, **classify**, and **categorize** it.

Wow, that sounds really interesting! - probably no reader is saying to them-self right about now.

But, not to worry, this discussion is not really going to be on the mechanics of it all, but rather why and how to think about this subject in relation to the martial arts.

Organization

Organization, in general, just means coming up with a scheme to be able to retrieve and understand pieces of information.

Another way to look at it is:

Without *organization*, one probably won't find what they are looking for very quickly. And, maybe never. And that is not good.

For example:

Let's say one is looking for a note about a thought they had a few years ago on kicking.

How would they find it?

If they were *organized*, they should be able to find it quickly. If not, who knows?

In short, *organization* is a major key to any serious thinker.

> *Opinion: There is a very interesting book called "Getting Things Done" by David Allen on the general subject of* **organization** *and its importance to having a clear and clutter-free mind that is open to new ideas and thoughts, while not being overcome with the baggage of day-to-day priorities. At minimum, It is worth a look at for the general concepts and strategies.*

So, what does all this have to do with the martial arts?

If one stops to think about it, a *system* of martial arts is basically an *organization* of the that art's *principles*, *rules*, thoughts, and movements.

Another way to look at it is:

A martial art **system** is the expression of **mind** and body in a specifically **organized** manner. Nothing more, nothing less. And, understanding this is key to not only understanding one's own art, but also potentially developing new arts.

In short, it is not whether there is **organization**, just how the information is **organized**.

> *Note: There is an overlap with the **Principles and Rules** and **Fundamentals** chapters.*

Classification

Classification generally means putting things together that belong together.

In other words, to group related things and distinguish them from other things that aren't related in the same way. Or, to draw lines between things by their differences.

> Note: There is an overlap with the **Opposites and Reverses** chapter.

For example:

Doing something to stop a strike may be *classified* as defense. Doing something to hurt someone may be *classified* as offense. Or, hitting with the foot may be *classified* as a kick. Hitting with the hand may be *classified* as a punch.

Sounds easy enough, but then the question arises:

Why do we do this?

In general, to get things organized in our *minds*.

Classification sets up a framework in our *mind* in which we can bunch things together; so that we may better compare, contrast, and analyze each item individually, or as a group, more *efficiently* and *efficiently*.

> Note: There is an overlap with the **Economy, Efficiency, and Effectiveness** chapter.

This classification concept sounds simple, and at times it can be; but at other times it can be difficult and almost confusing.

Why?

Two (2) major reasons:

First, things can be on a *spectrum*.

Note: There is an overlap with the **Spectrum** section of the **Opposites and Reverses** chapter.

And second, it depends upon how one is looking at something (*perspective*).

For example:

We have decided that we want to *classify* maneuvers as either defensive or offensive.

Starts out simple. Clearly a block that is designed to divert a punch is defensive, and clearly a punch that is designed to strike and injure an opponent is offensive. But, what about a punch that strikes an oncoming punch that not only stops the punch, but breaks the hand of the opponent in the same movement.

Where would we *classify* this type of maneuver?

This *classification* is a lot trickier.

Why?

Because it depends upon how we handle the analysis.

We can decide that the intent was defensive and *classify* the maneuver as such. Or, we can decide the intent was offensive and *classify* the maneuver as such. Or, we can decide not to decide and put the maneuver in both *classifications*.

> *Note: There is another option; not to put the maneuver in any* **classification**. *But this option was purposely overlooked due to fact that the example explicitly says we wish to* **classify** *the maneuvers.*

> *Note: There is still yet another option:*
>
> *Change the* **classification** *analysis to include a third option.*
>
> *In other words, add a new bucket for maneuvers that have both features equally and put it in that* **classification** *and/or with the other* **classification(s)**.

This type of analysis is basically binary thought. Binary thought goes like this:

Given two (2) groups (A and B) and something to put in those two (2) groups, there are only four (4) options; put the item in either A or B; put the item in both A and B; or don't do anything with the item (neither A or B).

As an example of binary thought:

Consider punching. One can punch with their left hand, they can punch with their right hand, punch with both hands, or don't punch at all. Those are the only options available.

> *Note / Opinion: Another way to look at this form of analysis is as how a computer would handle two (2) bits. Given these two (2) bits there are only four (4) possible outcomes: 00, 01, 10, and 11.*
>
> *In other words, both bits off, both bits on, or either bit on.*
>
> *The interesting thing about this type of analysis when brought to the real world, such as the punch example, is people tend to forget the nothing option (00). Don't forget to look at nothing (00) as an option. We tend to get so caught up in the something and our thoughts about it, we tend to forget the nothing.*
>
> *So, always take the time to consider the **opposite** of something - i.e. nothing.*

A common question can arise from all this is:

So, what's the point of all this *classification*?

Clarity of thought and action. Getting things clear in one's head provides a host of benefits.

For example:

If one teaches, clarity of thought allows one to better transfer those thoughts and movements to another. Having clearly grouped maneuvers and thoughts allows one to teach those maneuvers and *principles* to others in a concise, *effective*, and *efficient* manner.

And for personal benefit. Clarity of thought and action allows for better understanding of options and *strategies* when applied to self-defense situations.

*Note: There is an overlap with the **Principles and Rules** and **Fundamentals** chapters.*

*Opinion: **Classification** is an essential key to **organization**, and is also the foundation of any form of curriculum. Teaching others requires both clear thought and structure. This is nearly impossible without **organization** and specifically without some form of **classification**.*

While tangent thoughts, ideas, and maneuvers are excellent for developing and exploring new avenues; once those explorations bear fruit, it is in one's best interest to *classify* these new elements and add them to the *organization* of the existing structure in of both one's *mind* and potentially one's art.

Categorization

OK, we now have *organization* and *classification* to help us add structure to our thoughts and actions.

So, why do we need *categorization*? Isn't it the same as *classification*?

In many respects it can be. But, for the purpose of this book, we will be treating *categorization* with a special emphasis upon completeness.

Completeness of what?

Completeness of possibilities.

> Note: In American Kenpo lingo this action is referred to as category completion.

In order to understand this practice, one must first understand what a *category* is and how to use it.

For our purposes, a *category* is a defined boundary of thought, physical structure, or action where elements are grouped together because they share common characteristics.

In other words, a *category* can be considered a list of items that can be logically grouped together because they have something in common.

So, to make this more real let's start with something simple and then something a little more complex.

First, a simple *category*:

How many sides of the body can we strike with?

For this example, we will limit our *category* to left and right, because we have two (2) arms and legs. So, if we wanted to fill our **category** with all the possibilities, the **category** would be constructed as follows:

left side, right side, both sides together, or no striking at all. A total of four (4) combinations.

Probably, the next logical question that might arise would be:

What about the legs and arms, aren't they treated separately?

That depends upon our defined boundaries of the **category**. Are we considering top and bottom with left and right, or not?

For our example, if our answer is no, then the boundary is just left and right. But as an alternative, we could easily expand the definition to include top and bottom. And, that decision would complicate the **category**, possibilities, and expand the number of items in the list.

> Note: There is an overlap with the **Classification** section.

Now for a slightly more complicated example:

Let's create a category comprised of viable points of contact when striking with the hand.

In other words, how many potential, different contact points on the hand are **effective** when we decide to strike our opponent with our hand?

Let's go through the process of listing some of them:

Knuckles, half-knuckles, heel of palm, palm, and tips of fingers.

These are definitely the most common. But, then the following two questions arise:

Did we get them all? And, why did we do this?

> *Note: Some readers may have noticed that left and right is now purposely excluded from this new **category**. But again, this element could be added if we changed the defined limits of the **category**.*

Well, to start, the first question is the general answer to the second question. For our purposes, we did this to uncover all the possibilities, making sure that we didn't miss any items.

In other words, ensuring completeness.

By creating a **category**, one can then fill it with all the items that fit into it, and therefore make sure that one doesn't miss anything.

Another way to think about **categorization** is:

It is a technique to help one make sure that one doesn't miss any possibilities that might otherwise be accidentally overlooked.

> *Observation: If one takes this process to it's logical (and absurd) conclusion, everything (yes, everything) we do and think can be considered an item in one or more **categories**. And therefore, just an entry in a list to determine the completeness of the **category**.*

And, to answer the first question:

It depends upon the defined boundaries of the **category**.

For instance, does the **category** treat each finger as a separate item in the **category**? Or, are they grouped together as a single item? And, how about the knuckles. Does the **category** treat the front of the knuckles different from the back of the knuckles? And, each knuckle separately? Or again, are the knuckles treated as a single item? And to go further, will the **category** treat multiple contact points on the hand as individual items in the **category**?

If so, then how many different ways can one make contact with different combinations of fingers? One (1) finger, two (2) fingers, four (4) fingers, thumbs, finger(s) with thumbs, etc... Or, will we break this whole finger and knuckle conundrum into its own *category* and consider it all separately?

> *Opinion: Don't get lost in* **categorization***. While* **categorizing** *things is a very useful tool. Don't overlook or forget the fact that it is just a tool.* **Categorization** *can be easily taken too far and to the point where one loses the forest through the trees.*

The important thing to remember in all of this is:

One must have clearly defined boundaries in order to determine completeness of a *category*.

But, the really interesting thing about this exercise is the exposure of things probably not thought about before this exercise.

For instance:

Think about how this *categorization* exercise expanded from the beginning to the end. Was it anticipated that it would take this turn?

Probably not.

But, as the exercise concluded each reader's mind probably started considering other characteristics or properties to look at or consider.

This is one of the true powers of *categorization*: opening one's mind up to possibilities, avenues, and completeness of thought and action that might otherwise not be explored or considered.

> Note: There is an overlap with the **Spectrum** section of the **Opposites and Reverses** chapter.

Another way to think about **categorization** is:

It is a good way to expose **nuance** in action and thought. It can force one into examining things in ways that they may have previously not paid attention to or considered.

While **categorization** can be a tedious exercise, it can often spur on new thoughts, considerations, and subtleties that are frequently overlooked and missed upon less stringent analysis and examination.

> Note: There is an overlap with the **Nuance** chapter.

Further Exploration

There is one other thing that needs to be mentioned when working with *categorization*. And this topic is probably best explained using an example:

Let's consider a *category* that deals with blocks to the lower part of the body - a.k.a. downward blocks. These are blocks with the hand/fist pointing in a general downward direction, and are used to divert oncoming strikes primarily to the upper legs and groin area. Also, we will further restrict this *category* to not distinguish between sides (i.e. not distinguish left from right). Now that we have our category sufficiently defined, we can begin filling it with all the possibilities.

Upon examination, one should uncover that there are two (2) primary characteristics that can be called out in this *category*:

Whether the block is going toward the same side of the body as the arm (a.k.a. downward block) or the opposite side of the body (a.k.a. inside, downward block).

And whether the palm of the hand is facing upward (a.k.a. palm up) or downward (a.k.a. palm down).

With all these details laid out we can now determine how many blocks can be placed into this *category*. If done correctly, one should come up with the answer of four (4):

Downward/palm-up; downward/palm-down; inside, downward/palm-up; inside, downward/palm-down.

Some readers may have noticed something peculiar about the first item. One probably wouldn't or shouldn't do it.

Why?

Because it is an in-effective maneuver.

Again, why?

Because of limitations in how we are constructed.

In other words, our arms don't move effectively in that manner or motion, because of how we are physically built.

> Note: The nothing option was omitted from the list of possibilities. This was not an oversight. This was purposeful.

So, then the following questions typically arise:

What just happened here? Is this discovery exclusive to this example? What do we do with this discovery?

First, we uncovered motion that we should be aware of, but probably never execute "for real."

In other words, we pointed out a limitation of our physiology.

And second, obviously this is not the only example of our limitations. There are plenty more. But, one should certainly become aware of them, take note of them, and exclude them from practice.

> *Note:* In American Kenpo lingo this procedure is call purposeful omission.

> *Note:* To help with exploration in this area; here are some characteristics of our body to consider:
>
> A lot of our joints only bend in one direction, others in limited directions; our sight has a very small cone of focus and is limited to 180 degrees in total; our balance is very unstable in specific directions and more stable in others; our arms work with the forearms rotated in specific directions better than in others. Some of our muscles work better for pulling, while others for pushing; and our brains can only focus on one (1) item at a time. And when our brain context switches, it takes a little bit of time to fully focus on the new item.

Just as we have done in other chapters of this book, it is always good to look at things from the *opposite perspective*. In this case, not only look at things from what is effective, but what is also in-effective. And, *categorization* can help uncover these items in a very clear, concise, and detailed manner.

> *Note:* There is an overlap here with the **Opposite and Reverse** and **Perspective** chapters.

Final Thoughts

Although nothing can replace an active and fertile *mind* or just plain raw skill; those talents will only get one so far when it comes to longevity. What is just as important and vital to passing these potentially brilliant innovations, ideas, and skills down to others, long term, is making this information understandable, obtainable, and digestible to others.

And the only real way to do this is through some form of *organization*. Hopefully, the discourse presented in this chapter inspired some thoughts in helping to attain this critical goal successfully.

Even if one isn't concerned about innovative and/or revolutionary aims, one can still get further clarity and greater vision into their own art by simply knowing the methods discussed in this chapter. Comprehending *organization*, *classification*, and *categorization* and how they are used will definitely expand one's understanding and awareness of any structure.

And hopefully and more importantly, it is hoped that these discussions brought about more transparency and insights into how the configuration of any art was coalesced and shaped into becoming the art and what it is today.

> *Note: One thing to always keep in mind is that there is always some form of **organizational** structure, no matter how random it may appear to be.*
>
> *Even if there is a purposeful attempt at randomness, that is still an **organizational** structure.*

Part

XIV

Fundamentals

Overview

Quick, think of some words that describe a great martial art *system*.

Words like:

Effective, powerful, deadly, and efficient would be common. Even words like: elegant, beautiful, captivating, comprehensive, or mysterious might be used.

One word that is almost guaranteed not to be used:

Teachable.

Teachable?

Yes, teachable.

Why teachable?

Look at it from this *perspective*:

What good is the best martial art in the world if it can't be passed down to others? The founder of any *system* is supposed to be able to understand and perform their art. But, if that *system* is not able to be sufficiently conveyed to others, it will effectively die with the founder, or soon thereafter. Obviously, not the best-case scenario for any *system* and it's longevity.

So, without an effective means to teach an art, the final result will be the eventual demise of that art as envisioned by the founder.

In other words, if instructors of a martial art cannot successfully teach everything necessary about their art to others, how will that art survive? In reality, it can't.

> Note: There is still a case to be made by the founder that
> their art should NOT be taught to others. This case is
> purposely omitted from this discussion.

So at this point, the following question arises:

What does all this have to do with fundamentals? That is the
name of this chapter.

Well, let's look at all this from another angle:

Every martial art needs to express itself physically. The way in
which this is accomplished can vary dramatically; but every
single martial arts **system** has some form of physical expression
- with no exception.

Because of this fact, it is possible to look at and understand the
different means to this expression. And, to understand how a
martial art expresses itself physically leads one to uncovering
the keys to imparting that martial art to others.

In other words, how that martial art may be taught.

> Note: There are some extreme cases where a "martial
> art" expresses itself via psychological measures. That
> extreme case is purposely omitted. But, even in that
> instance the results are still expressed in some physical
> way. Usually by suppressing or avoiding the potential
> physical conflict - which is still ultimately a physical
> expression.

This still begs the question:

I still don't get it. Where are the **fundamentals**?

The **fundamentals** are what are distilled from understanding a
martial arts' means of expression. Things like **basics**, **strategy**,
training **drills**, and **fighting** methods can be extracted, detailed,
and used to teach the **system** to others.

Thus, understanding a martial art lies in understanding it's *fundamentals*.

> *Note: There is a case to be made for considering man-made weapons (such as sticks, knives, guns, etc.) in this discussion; but this chapter purposely excludes that specific topic from this chapter. Instead it will specifically consider only hand-to-hand.*

Leaving a permanent legacy is a prominent subject that has influenced and/or shaped many a martial art (and martial art instructor) since the inception of martial arts. And, every reader should be keenly aware of that fact.

This is worth repeating:

What good is the best martial art in the world if no one can learn it well enough to be good at it?

> *Exercise: Try to imagine how may martial art **systems** have become extinct or dramatically altered from their original **intent** throughout the centuries because they were unable to **effectively** and/or sufficiently teach the **fundamentals** of the **system** to others.*

Further Exploration

So, with the above understanding under our belts, there arises yet another directly related problem:

Education vs application.

Most likely, that statement elicits the following quandary:

What in the heck is that?

Look at it this way: Moving from a teaching environment to a realistic combat hardened readiness situation - or vice-versa.

In other words, think of it as a *spectrum* with education on one side and application on the other and how each element discussed fits into this *spectrum*. More towards education, more towards application, or squarely in the middle.

> Note: There is an overlap with the **Spectrum** section of the **Opposites and Reverses** chapter.

The vast majority of martial arts *systems* have proficiency of practitioners in the "real world" as their goal. But a few don't overly concern themselves with that objective. And, still others have the direct *opposite* concern; maximum "reality" with minimum "practice." But the vast majority of *systems* lay somewhere in the middle.

For example:

Compare Tai Chi Chuan to Jeet Kune Do in this regard.

Literally, Tai Chi Cuan takes the standpoint that one can apply the maneuvers in the "real world", but there is hardly any emphasis towards that end - at least not until after much practice in the art.

Whereas, Jeet Kune Do's approach is to just start fighting and work it all out over time and guidance. Two diametrically opposed approaches.

Which one is right? Or, are they both right? Or, are neither of them correct?

> Note: There is an overlap with the **Organization, Classification, and Categorization** chapter.

The answer is really not that important.

Not that important? Sounds very important!

Not really.

Why?

Because, it all depends upon the **principles** and goals of the art.

But what is important is that one understands all the potential permutations of the answers to the question and are able to formulate their own conclusions from them.

In other words, it's more important that one understands all the options and make up their own mind about the answer.

Another way to look at it:

it's not the destination, but the journey to the destination that is important.

So, working through the **fundamentals** of the **system** and how they align with it's **principles** and goals are the key to developing effective methods of conveying the **system** to others.

Opinion: So, another way to look at all this is:

One can be a great practitioner, a great instructor, or both. One should learn to become both if they wish their art to survive the test of time. And, one should insist their instructors do the same.

t is even arguable that having great instructors is more important than great practitioners, in this regard. Great instructors can produce great practitioners. But, often not the reverse. So, a balance of practitioners and instructors is essential to an art's longevity.

*All instructors should find a practitioner's strong suit and learn to discern and encourage great instructors, if that is there predilection. They may not be the best representation of the art physically, but if they can effectively convey its core **principles** and goals, they are just as an important element to the **system** as the top practitioners.*

Sport vs Combat

There still remains another major **perspective** that can dramatically alter our **fundamentals**, how they are taught, and how they are implemented. It can be coined **sport vs combat**. **Sport vs combat** can be thought of as the approach in which a specific art (or part of an art) is taught.

Is it taught primarily as a **sport**, or is it taught primarily for **combat**? And, what's the difference?

The vast majority of people reading this right now probably think they understand the difference.

But, do they really?

Sure, one can probably watch a video and say, that is a **sport**, or that is **combat**. But what are the tangible differences? And, can they be spelled out?

It is proposed here that there are two (2) primary factors that distinguish **sport** from **combat**. They are:

Intent and **rules**.

It is the combination of these two (2) elements that can be used to definitively determine **sport** from **combat**.

First, we all can agree that regardless of whether we are engaging in **sport** or **combat** that the ultimate aim we wish to achieve is victory. The only differences lay in the how and what we are willing to do to achieve it.

> Note: There is an overlap with the **Principles and Rules**. and **Economy, Efficiency, and Effectiveness** chapters.

Intent from the **perspective** of this book can be described as:

To what extent is one willing to go to defeat their opponent(s).

In other words, does one's victory potentially include any type of deadly force? If so, then one is definitely leaving the *sport* realm and definitively in the *combat* realm. If not, then one must consider the next factor.

Another way to look at this is:

Is the *intention* to achieve victory to such an extent that the opposing side can never compete again?

In other words, is the *intention* to defeat the opposing side permanently? Or, just for now. Big difference.

Rules from the *perspective* of this book can be described as:

What can't one do to achieve victory?

In other words, what stops the practitioner from doing things that they know will ultimately lead to victory? Another, very general, way to look at it is:

The more the *rules*, the further the art tends to get into *sport* territory and further from *combat* territory.

Again, this probing question arises:

What does all this have to do with *fundamentals* and how they are taught?

Well, back to *sport vs combat*.

If the *intent* of the art that is being taught / learned is designed more as a *sport*, then one will not be implementing maneuvers with the expectation to kill or permanently injure and/or perform maneuvers with the *intent* of deadly force. And, the *opposite* is true for *combat*.

This fact profoundly changes both what is taught and how it is executed. And, all this definitely impacts the *rules* that will be created around the *intent*.

> *Note: There is an overlap with the **Opposites and Reverses** and **Perspective** chapters.*

For example:

Sparring is definitely a **sport** and has **rules** and **intentions** to achieve victory without permanent injury to the opponent(s). Where **self-defense techniques** are **intended** for **combat** and work on a completely different set of maneuvers, **rules**, and **intentions**.

> *Note: There is an overlap with the **Basics**, **Self-Defense Techniques**, and **Fighting** sections in this chapter.*

This discussion should be kept in mind while moving forward through this chapter. And, one should keep in mind how the factors presented in this section effect how and what is actually taught within a **system**.

There is one large exception to this discourse that needs to be called out. And, that is:

The purposeful governing of skill and lethality due to personal, social, religious, and/or **spiritual** influence and/or beliefs.

For example:

Monks that train in the martial arts frequently take a sacred, voluntary vow not to purposely kill or permanently injure. They train with the proper skills, but have made a conscious decision not to use that ability when it comes to "real" conflict. This decision does not shift their training more towards **sport** and away from **combat**. It is a personal choice, and generally not one that is imposed or intended by the **system** itself. Although some systems may alter or exclude specific targets to help adhere to this decision.

In other words, it is the practitioner who makes the decision not to be lethal, not the art and it's taught abilities.

*Note: There is an overlap with **Mind** section of **The Human Element** chapter.*

Note: This decision of non-lethality is not exclusive to monks. Anyone can make this decision for them-self. Monks were specifically chosen because of the general and open understanding most people have about them.

Drills

Pretty much everything martial artists do outside of using their skills in an actual combat situation can be classified as a *drill*. Every type of *fundamental* mentioned in this chapter is in actuality a *drill*. At this point, the following questions often arise:

What about *forms*? What about *fighting*?

Yes, even *forms* and *fighting*.

If one is not using their skills in an actual combat situation, then in truth, one is practicing for the real thing; and therefore, carrying out a *drill*. We would all like to believe that some of the more aggressive and "realistic" *fighting* scenarios that some practitioners partake in are not *drills*. But, let's be honest with ourselves, they are actually *drills*.

> *Opinion: The above recognition is not a bad thing. It just is. And, we all should acknowledge this fact and use it to our advantage. Not try to make justifications and/or deny the fact of the matter.*

> *Note: There is overlap with the **Rationalization** chapter.*

> *Note: The most commonly used alternative names for **drills** are: exercises, warm-ups, work-outs, and just plain training.*

Conditioning vs Proficiency

OK, so we all perform various *drills*. But, let's not lose the tree through the forest. Probably the most important feature of *drills* is their purpose and goals.

In other words, what is it the *drill* is trying to impart upon the practitioner?

We started this chapter with viewing the *fundamentals* on the *spectrum* of *education vs application*, but there is another *perspective* to consider with *drills*:

Conditioning vs proficiency.

In other words, is the *drill* designed to improve one's physical health or skill level?

Every *drill* mentioned in this chapter (and those not) may be placed on this *spectrum*.

Note: There is overlap with the **Perspective** chapter.

Note: There is an overlap with the **Spectrum** section of the **Opposites and Reverses** chapter.

Note: Keep in mind that this point of view switch is just one other viewpoint. This does not mean there aren't any more **perspectives** or that they are any less important than this one.

At this point, the following questions may arise:

So what? Why is this important? Why should I care about this?

Because every *drill* should have at least one purpose and/or goal. And, a major key to determining that purpose is whether it is designed to improve the physical well-being of the practitioner, work toward teaching a skill to the practitioner; or both.

For example:

Are push-ups, sit-ups, running, etc. *drills* performed in one's art or training? If so, they are most definitely on the complete far end of the *conditioning spectrum*.

Why?

Because they have no direct correlation to learning one's martial art.

In contrast, a *form*, *self-defense technique*, or *fighting* tend to lean more heavily toward the proficiency end of the *spectrum*.

So, where does something like punching a makiwara board land on the *spectrum*?

Arguably, somewhere close to the middle.

Again, why?

Because punching builds *proficiency*, but the board and physical exercise also builds *conditioning* for the fist and self, respectively.

Observation: **Drills** *that tend to lean toward the* **proficiency** *end of the* **spectrum** *will also tend to be more specialized to that art. Where drills that tend to lean toward the* **conditioning** *end of the* **spectrum** *will also tend to be more common in nature - i.e. used across more* **systems***.*

The one big exception to this rule is **basics***.* **Basics** *can be very specialized to the art, but also tend to be more universal; just distinctive between arts.*

An interesting question arises about **basics** being the exception:

Why?

Because we all stand, block, and strike (a universal thing); but we all do it a little different, with big overlaps in the coarse movement.

Why again?

Because there are just so many ways the human body can move, in general. There are limits. So, although the specifics and **nuances** are relatively distinctive to our specific art, the rough maneuver is universal. It's just that there are so many factors to the specifics and **nuances** that there is an excessively large number of permutations of variations to the same movement.

Another way to look at it:

There are so many moving parts, no wonder there are so many different martial art **systems**.

There are literally hundreds, if not thousands, of different **drills**. Each one trying to accomplish something different. But in the end, each one is designed to improve the practitioner physically and/or improve the practitioner's skill.

*Opinion: The key to a good **drill** is a clear and narrow purpose. A **drill** should not try to be all things. Rather, it should be very specific in its goals, narrow in scope, and relatively easy to execute and/or understand.*

There is still one thing that needs to be made clear about this discourse:

Physical *conditioning* and skill *proficiency* can take on many different forms and is not limited to just the obvious cardiovascular or systemic specific improvements.

In other words, don't put self-imposed limits on your definition of these terms.

For example:

Weapon *conditioning* can be classified as a physical *conditioning*, but has nothing to do with cardiovascular improvement. Balance improvement can be classified as skill *proficiency*, but has nothing directly to do with improving a specific skill in the art. And, neither of these would fit the obvious interpretation of *conditioning* and/or *proficiency*. But both are valuable in their own rights.

Note: Weapon conditioning in this context is referring to the standard definition of hardening the weapon through repeated exposure to injury for the purpose of making the weapon harder to injure in the future. Such as in punching a makiwara board to harden knuckles or kicking a pole to harden shins.

Basics

Basics can be thought of as the atoms of the martial arts, or the letters of the alphabet of the martial arts language. They are the *fundamental* physical building blocks of all martial art *systems*.

In other words, without *basics* a martial art cannot exist.

Why?

Because any maneuver, movement, or action can be broken down into it's component parts and isolated as a *basic* or combination of *basics*. And, that is exactly the best way to describe or think about *basics*. The most elemental movement, position, or posture that can be demonstrated physically.

Finally, these individual elements can then be compounded together to form anywhere from simple to complex sequences. And, the potential for that compounding is virtually limitless.

> *Note: One mathematical way to think about the above description is through the use of factorials. Where each **basic** is a number of the factorial sequence.*

A formalized method of teaching *basics* almost always falls squarely within the educational *spectrum* of learning a martial art. This is because typically the setting is understood to be in an educational *environment*. Also a majority of the time, the *basics* are usually taught and executed from a series of "training" stances.

> *Note: There is an overlap with the **Spectrum** section of the **Opposites and Reverses** chapter.*

The rationale for this form of training is:

If the practitioner is removed from a high stress environment, they are more likely to be more mindful of proper execution, able to ask questions, and the instructor can spend the proper amount of time conveying information about the *basics*; for a more complete understanding of the actions to be performed.

There are a number of variations to this presented scenario, but the primary thrust of the above description is that the function of the situation is educational, it is known to be as such, and is for the purpose of learning very specific maneuvers and/or *strategies* of the *system*.

Basics are probably the most important elements of learning a martial art. Without a proper knowledge of standing, defending, and/or offensive maneuvering, what is one left with? Basically, the raw skill of the new practitioner.

But what about those *systems* that don't teach *basics* like described above?

Admittedly, there are *systems* that do not have this formalized method of learning *basics*. And instead, replace this form of training with one or more of the methods discussed in the other sections of this chapter.

Ultimately, it is up to the *system* itself to decide the proper way in which this form of education should transpire. But, the vast majority of *systems* tend to teach specific *basics* in a training situation. But, not all.

Note/Opinion: It is not the intent of this discussion to say that there needs to be a formal situation where **basics** are specifically taught. Just that a formal setting of teaching **basics** is the most common method.

This fact should not put any limits on one's thinking about **basics** and their education. Quite the **opposite**. The knowledge of this fact should only help give a foundation from which one can begin their exploration into this subject.

Note: Regardless of chosen method of education, all **systems** end up with the practitioner having the needed understanding and skill deemed necessary by that **system**.

Forms

Forms are very prevalent throughout most of the martial arts. Some arts have lots of them, but occasionally, some don't have any.

Most people have a preconceived notion of what a *form* is.

As a quick exercise:

Pause for a moment and consider your individual notion of a form. There is a good chance everyone is probably mostly wrong.

Mostly wrong?

Yes. Mostly wrong.

Why?

Because the majority of people assume *forms* are choreographed fights, a lot may think forms are simply moving *basics*, many feel that forms *catalog* or showcase one's art, some may even believe that they are very similar to dance routines, while still others have more complex explanations for forms. And, a few people may even consider forms to be totally useless.

Who's right?

All of them are mostly wrong.

> *Note: The most commonly used alternative names for* **forms** *are kata (Japanese), set (English alternative), or routine (English alternative).*

Forms are whatever the originator (or teacher) of the *forms* say they are - in relation to that specific *system*. And, nearly every art has a different way of thinking about *forms* and the role they play in the *system*.

Admittedly, there can be a lot of overlap in meaning with some of the "classical" martial arts. But the problem that most people face, and the reason they are mostly wrong, is because they try to apply their understanding of what a *form* means in their art(s), to other *systems*.

And that is, for the most part, tragically incorrect.

For instance:

Just because one's art interprets a *form* as a choreographed fight does not mean that this understanding translates to EVERY other *system*. And, if one applies their art's interpretation to the other *system*, the evaluation of that *form* will most likely fail dramatically.

Another way to look at this situation is:

One must first understand what a *form* means to that specific *system*, before trying to understand and critic a *form* and its movements.

For example:

Let's take the practitioner from the art that interprets *forms* as a choreographed fight. That practitioner observes a *form* where the other art views *forms* as moving basics.

What's going to happen?

Most likely, the practitioner will naturally make assumptions about "impractical" or "that wouldn't work" maneuvers from the observed *form*. The opinion created would most definitely be biased and probably fairly negative.

But if the roles where flipped (*opposite perspective*), the same would happen, but for a different host of reasons.

And, just for good measure, let's throw in a practitioner who comes from an art that thinks *forms* are useless (*perspective*).

They would most likely conclude both *forms* are a waste of time and counterproductive.

Who's right? Who's wrong? Who's to say?

Note: There is an overlap with the **Opposites and Reverses**, **Perspective**, and **Rationalization** chapters.

So, what does all this discussion on *forms* and their meanings show?

That *forms* are just another tool in the toolbox of martial arts. Some arts may use the tool daily, while others will never use it at all.

Also, *forms* are completely context driven. Their use or non-use is determined by the *principles* and goals of the martial art. And as such, opinions about *forms* are just as diverse as the *forms* themselves.

For example:

Tai Chi Cuan is primarily defined by *forms*. *Basics* are pulled and practiced from the *form*(s), but essentially the system is the *form*(s).

Where judo doesn't have any *forms* at all and is defined by is competition maneuvers - i.e. *basics* and *drills*.

Yet, both are centered around expression through exercise. Two radically different approaches with similar goals.

Another example:

Tang Soo Do has formal *forms*, but Savate does not have any. Both express themselves primarily through the use of legs and kicks, and again have fairly similar physical goals. But they also have completely different approaches to their view of *forms*.

Further Exploration

Aside from a *form's* meaning as it relates to a specific *system*, probably the best way to think about a *form* is as a story.

Like a story, a *form* can be short or long, narrow or broad in scope, or simple or complex.

And, continuing the analogy from *basics* as characters in the alphabet, a *form* can represent itself as words, sentences, paragraphs, and full-blown novels.

And like a story, there are really no hard and fast *rules* as to what composes a *form*. Some *systems* have very strict *rules* about what constitutes a *form*, some do not. Only that, essentially, a *form* has some manner of story to tell - whatever that may be.

Probably the most common expressions of *forms* are (in any order or combination): information hidden in plain sight, demonstration of the art's *principles and rules*, demonstration of the art's abilities, physical exercise, historical ancestry, and building a practitioner's abilities in the art.

> Note: Historical ancestry can be thought of as being like a hula dance. It is the physical telling of a story as a means to pass that story down to future generations.

Why is this important?

Because if one is to create a *form*, then one must first understand the story the *form* will tell.

In other words, what's its purpose and/or goals of the *form*? And, do those goals align with the *principles* of the art? Once those questions are answered, the rest will fall in line.

One undeniable aspect of *forms* is there propensity for historical longevity. Some *forms* have been passed down from generation to generation relatively unmodified for many, many years. Because of this, *forms* hold a special place in a large percentage of martial artists' hearts.

Forms have a very unique ability to represent the essence of an art in a very memorable and oft times beautiful way. Not that other *fundamentals* can't attain this same achievement; it's just that *forms* are the most obvious and frequently chosen *fundamental* used for this purpose.

Note: One other thing that must be observed is:

*In all reality, **forms** are just a specialized **drill** or may potentially be combined together with **techniques** into a single grouping. Although, **forms** may share many of the same attributes of that other **fundamental**, **forms** are separated out into their own **category** because they have many unique characteristics not shared with any of the other **fundamentals**; and because they have their own, unique historical roll within the martial arts.*

Education vs Application

There still remains this big question to answer about **forms**:

Where do **forms** fit into the **spectrum** of **education vs application**?

> Note: There is an overlap with the **Spectrum** section of the **Opposites and Reverses** chapter.

So, taking into consideration the previous discussions about **forms**, pause to think about the question for a moment Everyone will probably come to their own conclusion about this answer.

And, this time the conclusion about **forms** will probably be mostly right. The answer:

That depends upon context.

Why mostly right?

Because any time there is a predefined set of maneuvers, that eliminates the extreme far end of the **application spectrum**. Therefore, a **form** can never be considered entirely **application**. But it can be considered anywhere else in the range of possibilities.

> Observation: Admittedly, some readers may have gotten the complete right answer.

Most commonly, **forms** tend to fit more towards the **education** end of the **spectrum**. But, as always there are plenty of exceptions to this statement of generality. It is not a hard and fast **rule**, just a common trend.

Opinion: The interesting part of the answer is the why?

Why do **forms** *tend to be toward the* **educational** *end of the* **spectrum**?

The answer:

This is historical convention. And as such, the majority of martial arts practitioners are exposed to **forms** *in this educational light.*

And, most people tend to like to "go with the flow"; with very few "bucking the trend." It is just human nature that the vast majority of people try not to upset convention. Only a few mavericks leave conventional wisdom behind and strike out on their own and look at things from a dramatically different **perspective***. And, even fewer can do it successfully.*

In other words, its much safer to do what everyone else does. One has a better chance of success. But at the same time, this "safe" decision also runs the risk of becoming part of the noise and not distinct. Or, even worse, just considered a copy or variation of "x".

Self-Defense Techniques

How does one fight without really fighting? How does one get their sparring partner to do exactly what they want so that they may practice a specific set of maneuvers? How does one teach specific *strategies*, dangerous maneuvers, and solutions to specific defense situations in a controlled, yet relatively realistic *environment*? How does one teach *nuance*, *principles and rules*, and precision on an opponent?

All of these questions and many more can be answered by utilizing *self-defense techniques*.

> Note: The most commonly used alternative names for *self-defense techniques* are techniques (English alternative), "x"-step sparring (English alternative where x = a number), self-defense moves (English alternative), and "x" kumate (Japanese alternative where "x" = Japanese number).

To be fair, some readers may have answered any of the above questions with a totally different type of *fundamental*, such as:

Forms, *drills*, and/or *fighting*.

And, obviously, they would be right. Each of the questions could have been easily and correctly resolved with a completely different reply.

Why?

Because in reality *self-defense techniques* are just a specialized *drill* or a very short *form* designed to be executed with (a) partner(s).

And as such, *self-defense techniques* are judged in the same light as any of the other *fundamentals*, by most martial art *systems*. That is:

Some arts do a lot of *self-defense techniques*, some do a few of them, and some don't do them at all. It is up to the individual art to decide just how practical and effective, if at all, this **category** of **fundamental** is.

And, as most readers have probably gathered by now, the opinions cover the entire gamut.

One way to look at *self-defense techniques* is:

Self-defense techniques are a given response to a given attack. Thus, they tend to fall more on the *application* end of the *spectrum*; yet still retain some aspects from the *education* end.

> Note: There is an overlap with the **Spectrum** section of the **Opposites and Reverses** chapter.

Why *application* end?

Because even though there is a given response, the response is (typically) supposed to be "realistic". And, even though there is a given attack, the attack is (typically) supposed to be "realistic."

Thus, the major thrust (usually) is to approximate realism, yet still retain a controlled environment.

> Note: It is acknowledged that the "realism" may be ratcheted up in various ways such as: Not informing the practitioner of the given attack prior to execution; having a series of attackers with different, varying attacks; attacking from random angles; etc.

The main argument against all of this "supposed to be" stuff is exactly what it says - "supposed to be" is not entirely real.

Therefore, *self-defense techniques* can never be on the extreme far end of the *application* end of the *spectrum*; just like *forms*.

But they can very easily be pulled far into the *education* end of the *spectrum* through various means, such as: slowing the maneuvers, analyzing the *strategies*, breaking each maneuver down, working on precision, or not having a good or enthusiastic partner (or the practitioner not being enthusiastic).

> *Note: There is an overlap with the **Rationalization** and **Spontaneity** chapters.*

> *Opinion: **Self-defense techniques** are the nearly perfect touchstone for martial arts in general. Learning an art's attitude toward **self-defense techniques** and/or watching practitioners executing **self-defense techniques** can allow one to quickly assess a situation in mere moments. With a skilled eye, a massive amount of information can be gleaned in a matter of seconds from how and/or if a **self-defense technique** is performed.*
>
> *The same may be said about **forms**, but typically **forms** are much longer.*
>
> *"Show me your favorite or best technique" can be like opening a door not only into the art, but the **mind** and physical capabilities of the practitioner.*

The prior paragraph can often elicit the following sentiment:

So, this does not bode well for *self-defense techniques*.

But just because *self-defense techniques* can be easily pulled to the *education* end of the *spectrum* doesn't lessen their usefulness as a potentially effective *application* tool.

As mentioned at the beginning of this section, subtle and vital information specific to an art can be conveyed in a more realistic manner than using only *basics* or even *forms*.

In summation, *self-defense techniques* hold their own as one of the primary *fundamental* teaching aids that martial artists use to pass on their knowledge to others. And like most of the other *fundamentals*, can easily be shifted from one side of the *education vs application spectrum* to the other; based upon how they are handled, perceived, executed within an art and individual practitioner.

Fighting

Fighting is probably the most over-rated and under-rated type of training in the martial arts.

Stop! that sentence doesn't make any sense.

But it does make sense when put it into the context of all the different martial art **systems** out there and all their practitioners; combined with all their varying opinions.

Some practitioners feel that *fighting* is the highest form of training and no one can be a good martial artist if they don't partake in it.

While others believe that most *fighting* is really just a glorified game of tag with too many *rules* and is just a sport.

Who's right?

The reality lies somewhere squarely in the middle. As stated frequently within this chapter, *fighting* is just another tool in the toolbox of **fundamentals**.

> Note: The most commonly used alternative names for *fighting* are: kumate (Japanese), rolling, grappling, sparring, and freestyle.

Let's pause and take another look at the previous assertion.

Could one really become a good martial artist without *fighting*?

Certainly.

There are plenty of other effective *drills* that can fill the void and provide the same results as *fighting*.

And, what about *fighting* just being a game of tag?

One could argue the same about any other *category* of training in the martial arts.

Yes, *fighting* can be taken to the point of being an almost ridiculously ineffective tool. But again, any method of training could be taken to that level.

It's all about creating a proper training *environment* with proper motivations and defined results. Bad instruction on any *fundamental* will lead to bad results - regardless of the *drill*.

In short, it's not the *drill*, it's who's teaching it and how.

So, although *fighting* can sometimes be considered one of the most provocative methods of training. In all reality, it is just another tool for training. Nothing more, nothing less.

Further Exploration

Fighting is thought by some as the closest thing to true *application* that the practitioner can get outside of real combat.

Why?

Because one of *fighting's* purposes, by many *systems*, is to try and simulate combat as close to possible - just with more *rules*.

So, then the obvious question arises:

Why don't we just throw practitioners into a ring all the time to teach them *fighting*?

If one were paying attention to the question, it answered itself.

Teach is a synonym for *education*. And, without *education* what one has is just people guessing what to do, under pressure against an opponent. That situation is in stark contrast to the base goals of the martial arts.

And, while *fighting* can be adapted to be executed as an *educational* tool, most *systems* prefer to alter the *environment* and/or *drill* entirely to one that is more suited toward *education*.

So, next the following obvious question must be answered:

What are the base goals of the martial arts?

From one *perspective*, the martial arts can be thought of as the recognition and elimination of incorrect movements, while simultaneously improving the *economy, efficiency, and effectiveness* of our good movements. All accomplished within a specific approach and/or stylistic scheme.

In other words, the base goal of martial arts is to eliminate our bad habits in an effort to make us as physically and mentally *economical*, *effective* and *efficient* as possible; with minimal mistakes and maximum results.

This goal is accomplished through the implementation of various *drills* and lessons. *Fighting* being one of those *drills*. And, just allowing people to fight, without proper instruction and guidance, would not encourage or prompt the desired results.

> *Note: There is an overlap Economy, Efficiency, and Effectiveness chapter.*

> *Opinion: Like most of the other **fundamentals**, **fighting** starts out as an **educational** aid. But quickly moves more and more toward the **application** end of the **spectrum** as the practitioner progresses.*
>
> *The main problem with **fighting**, and not of the majority of the other **fundamentals**, is that once a practitioner becomes proficient, they tend to forget about the **educational** aspects of **fighting** and only concentrate on the **application**.*
>
> *Always keep the base goals in mind and remember to apply them to **fighting**.*
>
> *In other words, it's nice to have a free-for-all and train hard; but don't overlook and/or forget why we **fight** as martial artists.*

Breathing

Breathing - we all do it. And, we all do it automatically. And, almost all of us have certainly learned a few things about *breath*; it's importance, and perhaps a drill or two about controlling or manipulating *breath*.

There is a good chance that a lot of readers are starting this section with some hesitation, or just because it is the next section in this chapter. Maybe, not really thinking that anything will be learned from it. And admittedly, this might be right.

But, let's approach *breathing* from a different *perspective* than most discussions. Let's concede to and skip all the usual stuff about how important *breathing* is, how to control it, etc...; and discuss the physical mechanics of *breathing*.

> *Note / Opinion: There are a multitude of books on breathing, its importance, how to control it, etc. If one is interested in those aspects of breathing it is highly recommended that they read one of those books.*
>
> *The discussion in this section is not meant to downplay breathing and it's importance to the martial arts. It is just that nearly every discussion of breathing covers virtually the same information, over and over. And, this information is readily available to anyone of any interest in the subject.*

In order to *breath* in, one must relax a multitude of their core muscles. And conversely, in order to *breath* out, one must tighten some muscles. Understanding these simple facts are extremely important.

Why?

Because these simple facts can be used in your favor, or against you. In conjunction with two (2) other needed elements, *timing* and proximity, breathing can either be a benefit or exploited as a weakness.

Since we all must *breath*, during the inward part of the *breathing* cycle, there is a window of opportunity in which one is guaranteed that a number of the core muscles will be relaxed. And, relaxed muscles can either help with an offense (think speed), or can be exploited in defense (think getting hit).

> Note: There is an overlap with the **Opposites and Reverses** chapter.

This is where the other two (2) elements come into play.

Proximity just means that one is close enough to the opponent to make sufficient contact, so let's just assume that factor is taken care of. There are plenty of different *strategies* to solve for that problem, if needed.

That just leaves *timing*. Easy, right? Just wait until the opponent *breaths* in and then hit them as we *time* our own *breath* accordingly. And simultaneously, stay aware that the opponent might be doing the same thing.

There is a very good chance that almost all readers are shaking their heads about now in disgust and thinking:

No! Not so easy!

And that observation would be right.

> Note: There is an overlap with the **Timing** section of the **Economy, Efficiency, and Effectiveness** chapter.

Why? Why is it not so easy?

Because at that point in the conflict, all combatants are most likely in a heightened awareness state and either consciously or subconsciously ready for such a maneuver.

So, how does one solve for this dilemma? Once more, with *timing*.

Really? *Timing* again?

Yes, *timing* again!

Consider the following:

Have you ever had the wind knocked out of you? How did it happen? Definitely because you were *breathing* in. But, why at that time? And, why not at other times?

Because you were caught off guard.

In other words, you weren't ready and your mind wasn't expecting it and therefore your automatic reflexes didn't kick in to stop your *breathing* and tighten your muscles.

So, the question now becomes:

How does one replicate that situation?

There are at least two (2) ways; both of which requiring the proper *timing*.

Option #1 - Deception:

Deceive the opponent into actually believing that they are going to get hit at a specific *time*, but then delay that *timing* sufficiently to allow for their body to relax and begin *breathing* again. Then deliver the strike on the off-beat. How and where (i.e. which target) the deception is carried out is not important, just that the opponent believes it and further believes there is no follow up strike.

> Note: There is an overlap with the *Patterns* section of the *Economy, Efficiency, and Effectiveness* chapter.

Option #2 - Distraction:

Distract the opponent into not believing there is a strike. Again, delay the *timing* of the intended strike until the opponent relaxes and begins to *breathe* again. At which point deliver a *non-telegraphed* and/or obscured strike to the intended target.

> *Note: There is an overlap with the **Telegraphs** section of the **Economy, Efficiency and Effectiveness** chapter.*

> *Opinion: As a guideline, a typical delay in either scenario would probably be in the range of .5 seconds to just under a full second. But as the saying goes: "your **timing** may vary."*

> *Note: It is conceded that delivering a strike that the opponent never sees is also a very **effective strategy**.*
>
> *But for the purposes of this discussion, this type of strike would be considered as part of option #2.*
>
> *This is because the strike would be deemed obscured from the opponent's vision.*
>
> *But, if one wishes to create a new option for it, that conclusion does not conflict with the theme of this section (i.e. go for it).*

A few more things to take into account:

First, neither of these tactics are particularly unique, special, or exclusive in nature; they are just simple demonstrations of how to use *timing* to achieve the stated goal of keeping the opponent completely unaware of the fact that a strike is being delivered. And therefore, fooled into actually believing it is OK to breath, when it is not.

Second, always be aware that these same tactics can used by our opponent(s). Understanding the mechanics of how they work is essential to being able to overcome and/or defeat them.

Holding Your Breath

There is one very common problem that is so pervasive that it should be at least mentioned. That is: not *breathing* properly during the execution of maneuvers.

Usually, this constitutes the practitioner holding their breath during a series of maneuvers, and then continuing to *breath* after the full execution of maneuvers. Or, as another option, only breath periodically throughout the execution of maneuvers.

Regardless of the particulars, this problem is extremely common among new practitioners and should be spotted and corrected quickly. The problem is usually most noticeable when the practitioner is trying to put effort into multiple, sequential maneuvers, and usually with another practitioner; but sometimes also alone.

So, then the question arises:

How to fix this situation, if spotted?

There are a number of ways, but probably the most common approach instructors take is typically a variation on a discussion on how important *breathing* is and how to correctly coordinate it with the maneuvers. This instruction is then typically followed with the practitioner concentrating on *breathing* during execution of maneuvers, until this problem is discontinued.

This is by no means the only solution; but it is the most common.

*Note: Notice that there is no discussion on what constitutes proper **breathing**. This is purposeful because various martial arts have differing **principles** and theories on correct **breathing** methods and style.*

*Note/Opinion: It must be noted that some martial arts start with correct **breathing** habits even before starting to do physical maneuvers, and then work the physical maneuvers into the **breathing**. Some include correct **breathing** throughout instruction.*

These approaches tend to eliminate this problem before it even starts; and therefore, this section would probably seem odd and irrelevant to them.

Part

XV

The Human Element

Overview

There is an old martial art saying that goes:

You can't move, you can't fight. You can't breathe, you can't fight. You can't see, you can't fight.

That saying is incorrect - partially.

The first part is absolutely true. No movement, no fight.

The middle part is partially true. One can fight for a short time if not **breathing**. But the body eventually will need air in order to continue a sustained fight. Although, it is possible that a highly skilled martial artist might be able to start and conclude a fight without even **breathing**.

And, even though sight is an extremely important **sense**, once contact is made with your opponent, sight becomes far less important, and the fight can continue as long as needed. Absolutely not a completely true statement.

> Note: There is an overlap with the **Senses** section in this chapter;

What this saying is missing is the most important part of the body - the **mind**.

The **mind** controls everything we do. If we can shut the **mind** down, or just confound it, control of the rest of the body becomes highly impaired, if not stopped completely.

Taking these factors into consideration, the proper wording of this saying should be:

You can't think, you can't fight. You can't move, you can't fight. You can't breathe, you can't fight - [for very] long.

> Note: There is an overlap with the **Mind** section in this chapter.

So, why start this chapter with something like this?

Because this saying, understanding it and dissecting it, calls out some of the most seminal aspects of understanding the martial arts.

First and foremost, **the human element**. It demonstrates that in order to correctly analyze the saying, one must first understand human physiology.

Second, it demonstrates order of magnitude in **consideration**. The **mind** is the most important, followed by control of the body, and lastly sustaining the body with a needed ingredient.

Next, it lays out some fundamental **strategic** paths to victory over an opponent within conflict.

In other words, using our **minds** to study a potentially violent situation and determine paths to victory and/or avoidance; quickly and **effectively**.

And finally, it alludes to proficiency, **perspective**, and awareness of one's **environment**.

> Note: There is an overlap with the **Perspective**; **Environment**; **Economy, Efficiency, and Effectiveness** chapters.

Another way to look at this discourse is:

Stay grounded in **the human element**.

Martial arts is simply the study of **the human element** as it relates to conflict. And like most things, the more one learns about something, the better one understands it.

And, continual learning and understanding are some of the primary keys to success, longevity, and innovation within the martial arts.

> Note: The study of martial arts includes: both yourself and others, and is both physical and **mental**; and some may say it even has a **spiritual** aspect to it.

Students

Are all *students* created equal?

Sounds like a provocative question, but is it really? Look at it from these questions:

Should I teach all *students* the same regardless of mental and physical capabilities? Should I teach all *students* the same, regardless of *age*? Should I teach all *students* the most 'secret' of information my *system* has to offer? Or instead, should I spare that information for the most loyal and dedicated *students*?

Probably, not such a provocative question anymore.

Historical note: Back in the early to mid-1950's a group of martial arts masters happened to discuss these very questions. The answer they came to is as follows:

*There should be three (3) rings of **students**.*

*The first ring (and outer ring) would be the **students** that get taught as a standard **student**. They would learn the art that the general public would be privy to.*

*The second ring (and middle ring) would be the **students** that are conditioned as potential instructors of the art. They would be privy to more than the outer ring and taught with a slant towards teaching the art to others.*

*And the third ring (the inner ring) would be privy to all the information of the art. They would be considered the successors to the **system**.*

So, how does one tell them apart?

*As an outsider, one can't. Only the head instructor and inner ring **students** would be able to discern one type of **student** from the other.*

Everyone else would be oblivious.

And to carry this thought pattern even further:

What about the **student** that is just a casual practitioner? A student that just wants to learn to defend them-self and not become a proficient martial artist. Or, the **student** who is taking martial arts because their parent(s) feel it would be good for them.

The massive question that then arises is:

Does any of this effect what and how one teaches their art?

> *Note: There is an overlap with the **Final Thoughts** section of the **Nuance** chapter.*

The knee-jerk answer is:

Yes! Of course, this affects what and how one teaches.

But, hold on a second. Before we answer the question, we first must stop and think about what type of studio they are running (if any).

Does the studio teach to the general public, or privately? Does it teach groups of people, or give classes to individuals? Does it teach children, or only adults? Or, does it teach a combination of all the above situations? The answer to these questions will undoubtedly heavily influence the final answer.

This book cannot possibly hope to answer the above questions and cannot solve for every permutation of the answers that may be given. But what can be done is expose one to these important questions (for consideration), give some general advice, and potentially guide one into coming up with their own conclusions.

Probably almost every person reading this book already has some form of curriculum that they currently teach or has been exposed to. So, the question to ask is:

Does this curriculum answer all the presented questions to my satisfaction?

If not, what should be done about it - if anything? And, how should it be done?

If one has the luxury to teach privately, then the one (1) big piece of advice is:

Find out the goals of the new *student*; combine that with their skills, proclivities and predispositions; and tailor the instruction to meet both their needs and the *system's* goals and requirements.

In other words, learn to teach in a variety of different ways and with a variety of different progressions, based upon the individual *student*. This sounds tedious and difficult, and it is. But, learning to be dynamic, versatile, and able to meet challenges is one important aspect of learning to be an instructor / master of the arts.

If one primarily teaches in a commercial setting, then the challenge is to try and make the curriculum as transferable to as many people as possible, while also potentially allowing for special treatment for exceptional individuals on both ends of the *spectrum*.

> Note: There is an overlap with the **Spectrum** section of the **Opposites and Reverses** chapter.

This approach has its own, unique set of challenges, such as:

Many different age groups, new *students* entering the class, *students* of different levels in the same class, individual *student* to instructor time, and scalability of number of *students* per class, to name a few.

Some simple ways to solve for these issues:

Create multiple paths for advancement in the *system*; create a circular curriculum, which repeats itself frequently; offer private instruction; have multiple instructors on the floor at the same time; frequently split and merge the class together, based upon what is being covered and the dynamics of the class; and offer classes that cover specific subjects at specific times, while allowing for a general class.

It is fairly obvious that this section presents a large problem that can be solved in many different ways; each having strengths and weaknesses. But, no one can deny the existence and importance of the problem.

The only question is:

is it solved well enough for you and your *system's* expectations and goals?

Age vs Age

Take a moment to consider the following proposal:

All martial arts have two (2) primary **perspectives** when it comes to **age** - physical **age** and time in the martial arts. Physical **age** is the length of time one has been alive, and time in system is the length of training the practitioner has in the martial arts.

Disagree with this assessment?

Ask anyone their **age** and they will be able to answer, immediately.

Ask any martial artist how long they have been training and they can give a specific response (or start year), immediately.

Even from the practitioner's **perspective**, they effectively have two (2) **ages**.

OK fine, two (2) **ages**, but why link these two **ages** together?

Because, the interesting thing about both **ages** is that they are treated, in many respects, very similarly in the martial arts. But at the same time, very differently.

For example:

If a three (3) year old and a fifty (50) year old started training, wouldn't both individuals basically start learning the same things, at first? And then, as they advanced, they would learn more and more about the art, right?

Certainly.

The major difference is only the rate of progression. Where the three (3) year old might take ten (10) years to learn what the fifty (50) year old learns in a year or two (2). In the end, eventually both individuals will arrive at the same place in the art, just at varying lengths of time.

The same, but different.

But, isn't this true for everyone? Isn't everyone intended to arrive at the same place in the art, but at different lengths of time?

This is true.

Everyone will advance in a martial art at their own pace. But what about the individual who is taking an extraordinarily long time to advance? How does one handle that situation?

The first question any *style* has to ask itself about this subject is:

Does it even handle this situation?

Or better yet:

Does it even want to handle this situation?

Without hesitation, some arts answer the above questions as a resounding, no.

Their approach is:

The art is the art and it is taught a specific way, and that is it.

While, others take a decidedly different approach and are very accommodating to persons of all physical ages.

Regardless, it is up to the instructors of the martial art to decide how to answer the questions.

> *Opinion: There is no absolute right answer to the questions posed. But every instructor should be aware of and understand how these questions are answered, from their art's perspective.*

The real interesting part of the answer is:

How?

If one's art wants to deal with an individual who is definitely going to take a lot longer than the average adult to progress, how is it handled? Does the curriculum actually have to change for physically younger individuals?

> *Note: The above answers typically apply equally well to special needs individuals. Special needs individuals are purposely not discussed in this section, but similar adjustments (if not many more) will need to be made to handle such individuals. And, these adjustments are generally done on a person-by-person or need-by-need basis.*
>
> *Also, special needs situations may require special training and/or insight in order to achieve success.*

We all can agree that one must handle children, teens, and adults differently when it comes to learning the martial arts. Some studios start with children as young as three (3) years old. One is definitely not going to teach a three (3) year old how to effectively kill another three (3) year old.

So then the question arises:

What does one teach them to fill the gap of time before they are ready to learn this information?

The primary answer comes in the name of the chapter - **Fundamentals** and the main section - **Drills**.

Without question, everyone needs to learn the proper physical expression of their art. Even if certain mental aspects (and even physical aspects) of the art are delayed, the fundamental physical aspects can be improved and perfected through various *drills* designed to improve coordination, dexterity, and proper execution.

In short, *drills* are an excellent remedy for this scenario. Use them judiciously.

> Note: There is a potential overlap with the *Nuance* chapter.

Now to look at all of this from a different *perspective*:

One main problem that can arise with this scenario of various *ages* learning an art is:

Rank.

Remember that it was stated there are two (2) types of *ages*.

The question of which one is dominant will arise at some point. Physical *age* or time in *system*? And with this will also arise some other questions, such as:

Does a child even get a black belt?

If so:

Is a child black belt equivalent to an adult black belt?

And:

How is the child supposed to treat an adult of a lower rank?

All very real and potentially sticky questions.

> *Opinion: There should be very clear answers and procedures to handle these and other questions of similar nature. And, these practices should be made extremely clear to all practitioners - young and old alike.*

How to answer and handle all of this is up to the individual martial art and sometimes, even the individual instructor.

But without exception, every art should be aware of and have definite answers to this dilemma. Even if it is only to deal with the situation spanning multiple martial arts.

In other words, how your practitioners are expected to deal with other practitioners of all ages (both ages) from other arts.

Body

Consider the following:

If you were five (5) feet one (1) inches tall and weighed one-hundred and ten (110) pounds would you take up sumo wrestling?

How about if you were six (6) foot tall and weighed two-hundred and fifty (250) pounds?

Fairly easy answers. But, stop and ponder this:

What is at the root of the answers?

Physical differential in relation to **strategic** initiative.

In much simpler words, everyone is different and every martial art is different, and sometimes the combination of the two (2) differences don't really mesh.

Another way to look at it is:

Taller people tend to like to kick more; stouter people tend to like to grapple more; thinner people tend to like to move around more; older people tend to like to move slower.

> *Note: There is a mental facet to this decision also. Desire, hopes, dreams, attitudes, and beliefs. But, these aspects are purposely being overlooked at this time.*
>
> *See the sections on **mind** and **spirituality** for more on this subject.*

The overall answer to the above situation is fairly obvious:

The person's **body** type and/or **age**.

We tend to try and gravitate toward an art that is most suited to our *bodies*. Where some *systems* claim to be suitable for all shapes, sizes and *ages*; others tend to have specialties.

What is important about this subject is comprehending the peculiarities, if any, of the specific art; and making sure that the practitioners of that art comprehend what limitations or problems may arise from a bad fit.

In other words, the small person taking up sumo wrestling isn't impossible, it's just not very practical. And, that person should be aware of this fact.

> *Note: There is an overlap with the* ***Students*** *and* ***Age vs Age*** *sections of this chapter.*

Another completely different way to look at the subject of our *bodies* is:

There are many physical limitations we all share; there are some limitations that are specific to different types of *bodies*; and there are personal tendencies that are very specific to us as an individual.

One must learn to differentiate between these peculiarities and not conflate personal likes and limitations with relatively universal limitations of the human *body*.

Like any aspect of the martial arts, having a clear and comprehensive understanding of the human *body* is essential.

Using Energy

Probably a good number of readers saw the title to this section and thought to them-self:

I wonder if we will get into the mystical or unexplainable areas of internal *energy* and how the martial arts implement and use it? Or something in that range of thought.

Sorry to disappoint; *energy* usage is not very hard to explain and it's not mystical or magical in any way.

The mere fact that one is breathing, moving, reading, thinking, etc. expends *energy*.

Every time one touches another person (or anything) they are transferring some small amount of *energy* into them (or it). And, this *energy* is not some strange force, it's just force (*energy*) from the point of contact and motion.

For example:

Put your finger on the surface of some still water.

What happens?

Waves are created.

How did that happen?

Simply explained:

Some of the *energy* spent moving the finger to the water is transferred into the water, and that *energy* was used to create the waves in the water.

If one varies how the water is touched, they can change the effect they have on the water and potentially anything inside the water. One could just disturb the surface or effect the water at deeper levels; It all depends upon how one makes contact with the water. Faster, slower, deeper penetration, amount of surface contact; all of these and more will affect what happens to the water and how deep the effect will be within it.

In essence, it's no different with the human body.

> Note: This **energy** transfer discussion is applicable to any physical item, with some small differences, but this discussion is purposely limited to the human body.

So, to continue with the previous example:

Try to imagine the core of the human body as a big bag of water. And, as one strikes the bag in different ways, try to visualize how the **energy** from the strike either dissipates at the surface of the bag or may be directed into the bag at different angles, speeds, items within the bag, etc.

This can be accomplished by changing how one hits the bag (a.k.a. method of execution), how much surface area one allows to make contact with the bag (a.k.a. the weapon formation), and how deep they push their way into the bag (a.k.a. contact penetration), just to name a few variables.

Learning how each of these alterations effects how the **energy** is transferred into the bag and what effect it has on the bag and the items within the bag (a.k.a. targets) is one of the major keys to understanding how to manipulate one's **energy** in specific ways to get the effect (and damage) desired.

The real important parts of all of this **energy** manipulation talk is understanding that **energy** is very explainable and understandable; the real challenge comes in determining where, what, and specifically how one is transferring their **energy** within the bag or on the bag (a.k.a. body).

This requires a knowledge of both how to hit (a.k.a. methods of execution) and what to hit (a.k.a. **anatomy**).

> *Note: There is an overlap with the **Anatomy and Kinesiology** section in this chapter.*

To put it another way:

Is one trying to deflect or injure, break or crush, scratch or tear, rupture or puncture, detain or manipulate or something different entirely?

Each of these effects are accomplished by different methods of execution, different weapon formations, different amounts of surface contact, and different penetration depths, angles, and combinations of the above.

The skill is in learning what each of the variables (and more) does and how one can control the effect by controlling them-self and their *energy*.

> *Opinion: Stop thinking of **energy** as some mystical, magical force that only deep, dark masters can manipulate effectively. **Energy** and how to use it effectively is very easily explained.*
>
> *There is just skill in learning how to properly use it to create the effect one wants on the opponent.*

Senses

One's senses are essential to their execution of the martial arts.

All of their senses.

The main purpose of this section is to cover each sense, it's strong points and weak points and what order of importance each is to the martial arts.

First, most important, most obvious, and with very little to no argument; is sight.

Without a doubt, one's sight will be the most used sense in almost any conflict. It allows one to determine their external *environment*; opponent size, count, direction, and distance; and potentially intent, to name a just few of its most important strengths. But it can be fooled, misdirected, or bypassed fairly easily.

Our vision is limited in direction and very limited in focus. We essentially have a cone of vision in which we can see, and in that cone a very small spot in which our focus is directed. The rest of our vision is peripheral, or out of focus.

In that "out of focus" area we can see primarily movement, general shapes, and most colors; but not much more than that.

The reason why we think we see our entire cone of vision in focus is because our eyes dart around and focus on important spots very quickly and our *mind* fills in the focus for constant elements automatically; giving us the impression of complete focus.

Our eyes use movement in conjunction with our other senses to determine the important parts of our external *environment* to focus on.

> Note: There is an overlap with the **Environment** chapter.

With our cone of vision comes the reliance upon distance. The closer to the eyes, the smaller the cone of vision; and vice-versa.

Therefore, if one wants to have large parts of their body outside of the opponent's cone of vision, get close.

But, also keep in mind that the same is also happening to you, from the opponent's **perspective** (**opposite**).

> Note: There is an overlap with the **Opposite and Reverses** and **Perspective** chapters.

Also, we can't see through most solid objects or in the dark.

Therefore, it is relatively easy to obscure something (like a natural or man-made weapon) from view.

Finally, we can use these two characteristics in combination and put something in front of the eyes at varying distance to obscure more or less of one's vision.

Understanding these simple facts and others, from both a positive and negative **perspective**, is the key to understanding how to **effectively** use or creatively overcome the sense of sight.

> Note: One needs to consider the fact that there are a large number of circumstances where sight can be either minimized, eliminated or unnecessary.
>
> In these situations, one would naturally switch to relying upon touch to effectively compensate for the missing or impaired **sense**.

Next, and arguably the second most important sense, is the sense of touch.

Why arguably?

Because if there is no direct contact with the opponent, then hearing would be the second most important sense.

But, once contact with the opponent is initiated, touch becomes the most important sense.

Again, Why?

Because touch can be used to determine motion, it's speed, direction, and potentially **intent** by the opponent - just like sight. And in many cases, touch can be a good replacement for, or better than sight.

This is so commonly known, that many **systems** have **drills** that train practitioners on the proper use and exploitation of touch.

The major downside of touch is that it can be limited in scope on the opponent's body.

How?

A properly trained opponent may be skilled at isolating different movements in such a way that the area that is in contact doesn't feel or is fooled by the new movement from a different part on the body.

In short, much like sight, touch can be fooled, misdirected, or bypassed.

> Note: There is an overlap with the **Fundamentals** chapter.

> Opinion: a very famous **drill** that is designed to develop the sense of touch is called "sticky hands". If you have not heard of it before, it is recommended that you at least become familiar with it's execution and goals. This may open doors into your own exploration of the use of touch in training **drills**.

There is one other feature of touch that can be often overlooked:

It is the fact that we have hairs all over our skin and those hairs can detect changes in air pressure and movement of air fairly well; much like a cat's whiskers. Sometimes one can "feel" the opponent without seeing or hearing them by sensing these small differentials in the air. What may seem like supernatural senses can sometimes be explained by this innate ability of our outer layer.

> Opinion: Everyone should become keenly aware of these often overlooked or misunderstood features of our senses. They can be honed and used just as effectively as the more prominent characteristics.
>
> Plus, these minor and less-known characteristics could also be used just as easily and **effectively** against you.

The third, and sometimes second, most important sense, is the sense of hearing.

Hearing is most often used in conjunction with sight to inform it where to focus attention.

But it can also be used for other aspects of defense, such as:

To determine size, direction, distance, count, or fatigue of (an) opponent(s).

And, misdirection is probably the most commonly known problem with hearing.

Almost everyone has seen a movie or show where an object was thrown to make a sound to mislead the opponent as to location.

But there are other skills that may be developed with hearing that are not as obvious.

For instance:

Hearing can be used to determine success of injury on the opponent. Think cracking, air expelling, or grunting to name a few.

Finally, smell and taste.

These two senses are directly linked because taste is often enhanced by smell.

Probably the most useful way in which smell can be used in defense is determining direction (and potentially distance, count and who) of the opponent based upon wind.

But like all our other senses, smell (and taste) can be fooled.

> *Factoid: Smell is arguably the most linked sense to memory and mood. This is because the olfactory bulb is part of the brain's limbic system, the part of the brain closely associated with memory and feelings.*

One last thing that was somewhat glazed over is combining senses.

One should take the time to understand how the senses are used in tandem and explore other possibilities in which combining senses can add to one's repertoire of skill sets and overall awareness.

Also, the more senses that are engaged, the harder it may be to deceive.

In other words, the more one is properly paying attention with more of their senses, the harder it may be to be fooled, compared to only relying upon a single sense.

Anatomy and Kinesiology

Anatomy and kinesiology. Fairly big words. So, definitions are certainly in order.

Anatomy can be defined as:

1. The study of the human body's structure and composition.

Kinesiology can be defined as:

1. The study of the mechanics of how the human body moves.

If one is a martial artist, one is (or should be) also most assuredly an *anatomist* and a *kinesiologist*, to some degree.

Understanding the physiology of the human body and how it moves are without question essential elements of the martial arts.

Having knowledge of the structure and composition of the human body is key to understanding how to exploit it, injure it, and/or defend it. And, the same can be said about how we move.

Opinion: It isn't entirely necessary to learn all the medical and/or scientific names for every part of the body or mechanism of motion.

What is necessary is understanding where, what, and how these components are structured and how they fit into the proper function and structure of the body and motion.

But learning this information does go a long way at showing the dedication and deeper understanding of these areas of study.

So, then this sentiment/question arises:

Are you saying I have to study all of this science stuff to be a good martial artist?

No. Not at all.

Even if one just acquires a cursory understanding of the body and motion from learning where and how to exploit specific physical characteristics, one is still learning *anatomy and kinesiology* - just not directly and as a separate study.

So, even if science isn't really "your thing", one can still derive the benefits of these areas of science by learning some of the basics that can help one in achieving their goals.

Anatomy

From one of many martial art's *perspectives*, human anatomy can be construed as a collection of targets that are exploited and/or defended. And, this aggregate of targets can be broken down into a finite number of *categories*, based upon physical similarity.

As one example, the targets can be *categorized* as follows:

skeletal, muscular, organ, vascular and nervous systems.

Each of these *categories* has a very specific set of characteristics that should be studied. That study is left up to the reader to accomplish.

But what will be covered here is merely what comprises each *category* and some basic facts.

This overview is intended to be construed as a "getting started" example into one method of how to approach the subject of human anatomy.

> *Note: It is not expressed how the **categories** where created. This is purposeful, because it is only of many ways this could be accomplished.*

> *Note: One may arguably consider the brain as a separate **category**, outside of organ; due to it's uniqueness and importance; but this **category** is purposely omitted from this section and delayed until the next section of this chapter.*

> *Note: There is an overlap with the **Organization, Classification, and Categorization** chapter.*

The skeletal *category* is comprised of the bone structure of the human body and the joints that connect two (2) bones together. The skeleton is what allows the body to stand, have structure and aid in support the other *categories*.

Bones can be bruised, cracked, chipped, broken, crushed, ground, and powered.

But bones can also be strengthened (through calcification) and weakened (through lack of use and / or ailment).

The joints of the skeleton can be immobilized, locked-out, hyper-extended, and broken. One (1) item that falls into this list that is not completely obvious are teeth.

> *Note / Opinion: The study of joints, how they work, and how to exploit them is a very large subject within the martial arts. It is highly recommended that one gets a least a competent understanding of joints in relation to the martial arts. This subject can often be a complete study unto itself.*

The muscular **category** is comprised of both the muscle and tendon material within the human body. These are essentially specialized tissues that coordinate the many moving parts of the human body. They work hand-in-hand with both the brain and nervous system to accomplish this goal.

These elements can be bruised, punctured, ripped, torn, cut, and detached.

They can be strengthened through exercise and weakened through lack of the same.

The organ **category** is comprised of both internal and external matter of the human body.

Elements of the human body that fall into this category are: eyes, skin (nails, hair, and external ear), internal ear, groin (and anus), and all internal organs. These are the components of our body that basically keep us alive.

They can be scratched, bruised, punctured, ripped, torn, cut, ruptured, crushed, and removed.

Organs can't be strengthened to any degree of relevance.

The vascular *category* is comprised of the lungs, blood vessels, and glands of the body. These elements are primarily used as transport mechanisms to feed the body with or of the essential components of life or relieve it of waste.

They can be pinched, cut, ripped, torn, clogged, and punctured.

The vascular system can't really be strengthened.

The nerve *category* is comprised of the electrical conduits of the body. These elements are the primary signaling mechanism of the body. They work in conjunction with the brain to make everything work.

They can be severed, cut, interrupted, and confused.

The unique thing about the nervous system is that it really can't be strengthened, but it can be deadened. Deadening a nerve renders the nerve impervious to exploitation, but also any feeling.

> *Note: The discussion of exploitation and injury within each* **category** *is not intended to be a complete list. Rather a list of the most common possibilities that should be expanded upon by the reader.*

Kinesiology

So, why is the understanding of human physical mechanics important?

Because understanding how the human body moves and operates can unlock keys to understanding it, perfecting it, and also ways to effectively take advantage of it.

For instance:

Understanding the dynamics of how we walk can expose vital or weak points in the motion that if disrupted can be catastrophic to the act being successful.

In other words, examining how we walk can lead to ideas in how to stop others from walking, making them fall, or become unbalanced while trying to walk.

But this can only come about through examining the maneuver, generally understanding how it works, and then experimenting with ways to exploit it.

This is *kinesiology* in action.

From the *opposite perspective*:

Understanding the dynamics of walking can also be used to finding imperfections in the maneuver and therefore perfecting the maneuver.

And, why would one want to do this?

To become more *efficient*, more *effective*, and more *economical* at the maneuver.

In other words, to detect and eliminate problems or inefficiencies in the motion.

Again, why would one want to do this?

Because that is one major goal of many martial arts:

To become better at what one does; remove the inefficient, ineffective, or unnecessary motion; and use that improvement and understanding to one's advantage and success in self-defense situations.

> Note: There is an overlap with the **Opposites and Reverses**, **Perspective**, and **Economy, Efficiency, and Effectiveness** chapters.

One crucial element that needs to be called out about this discussion is that this practice can be employed with any human motion.

In essence, this is a fundamental way in which martial arts works.

We learn to understand how we move and then either employ it to improve our motion or use it learn to take advantage of the motion in others.

And, all of this is done to improve our chances of success in potentially life or death situations.

An example of this study in action, is:

Judo or Sumo. Judo and Sumo primarily work on understanding balance and weight distributions and then learning how to take advantage of that understanding in others, while simultaneously trying not to let others take advantage of it in you. Judo is exceptionally good at understanding key balance points in both stationary and moving opponents and employing throws and take-downs to disrupt that balance.

> *Note/Opinion: Some **systems** use **kinesiology** extensively throughout their art, while others use it superficially; but all use it either directly or indirectly, knowingly or unknowingly.*
>
> *For example:*
>
> *Take an animal style.*
>
> *How does that style mimic the animal?*
>
> *By studying that animal's motions and then replicating them in humans.*
>
> ***Kinesiology.***
>
> *It may not be explicitly called out as such within that style, but that's what the process essentially is doing.*

Continuing with the above example:

The understanding of balance is done in very specific ways that are beneficial to Judo / Sumo and their goals and *rules*.

This does not mean that one cannot use the same understanding in other ways and in other arts that better suit other specific goals and *principles*.

This is vital to understand:

Just because one has learned to understand a specific motion or aspect of human motion, doesn't mean there is a singular way to use that understanding.

There are many.

What dictates how that information is used are the underlying goals, *principles*, and potential *rules* employed in that understanding.

In other words, there are many creative ways in which the understanding of motion can be used and just because one way was chosen for a specific art, does not mean that this is the only way that information can be used.

Opinion: One way in which the above paragraph can be interpreted is:

*Do not get locked into or blinded by a specific method of employing **kinesiology** on a specific maneuver, for a specific art. Take the time to explore other options and/or learn how others have used that same information differently and potentially to different results.*

---

*Note: There is an overlap with the **Principles and Rules** chapter.*

---

*Recommendation: A good book on kinesiology, for those so inclined, is: **Anatomy of Movement** by Blandine Calais-Germain.*

Mind

Probably the most important thing one must understand about the human brain is that it is just like any other muscle in the human body.

So, what does this mean?

If one were taught a new defensive maneuver, offensive maneuver, or self-defense technique would they have it perfected after executing it once? Definitely not! They would practice it hundreds, if not thousands of times in order to master it.

The same is true with the *mind*.

For example:

Just because one reads this book does not mean that they now "think like a martial arts grand master." All the information presented in this book must be reviewed and thought about many times and for long periods before it becomes engrained in one's psyche.

Just like the physical maneuvers each of us practices regularly.

Probably the most asked question about learning non-physical information about the martial arts is:

How does understanding and studying all of this stuff help my martial arts?

Well consider this:

What is the one thing that controls one's actions both physically and non-physically?

The **mind**. And if one's **mind** does not accept, truly understand, or misinterprets the information that they are presented with, what will happen?

The quick answer is that they will suffer physically in some way or another. Either they won't practice correctly, they will allow mistakes to creep into their actions, or they just won't practice at all.

But, take a moment to consider the **opposite**.

The better one understands, the more they accept, and more engrained the information, the more motivated they will become, the more they will practice correctly, and the more natural their physical maneuvers will feel and be executed. Plus, they will find it more natural to find options and alternatives to those physical motions.

All because the **mind** becomes comfortable, accepting, and in control of the information.

> Note: There is an overlap with the **Opposite and Reverses**, **Spontaneity**, and **Nuance** chapters.

> Opinion: Even if one rejects all sections of information presented in this book, they will still have information directly related to their martial art that needs to be understood and absorbed.
>
> Without exception, all martial arts have a framework of information that all practitioners of that art must understand and master.
>
> And, the **mind** is the thing that controls it all.

So, what does this all mean?

It means that information is not separate from the martial arts, it is an integral element.

And, every martial art has critical information that must be studied, learned and mastered. And, just improving the physical aspects of a martial art is for people "who just want to defend themselves" - not advanced martial artists.

In order to master and teach a **system**, one must truly understand the depths of information that their art wishes to convey to the world.

In short, one must train their **mind** as intensely as they train their body.

Opinion: One thing everyone should consider about their training is whether their art is a good fit for their aspirations and objectives.

Unlike the days of old where the art one learned was based upon their family; in today's society one can choose their art and even change it at will.

Therefore, one should stop and assess the art they are training in to make sure that it is congruent with their convictions and character. And if not, consider moving to an art that better suits their disposition and/or physical constitution.

And yes, it is understood that this opinion is considered almost heretical in most martial arts.

Behavior

Our society expects us to act within a certain *spectrum* of *behavior*. And for the most part, we all do.

> Note: There is an overlap with the **Spectrum** section of the **Opposites and Reverses** chapter.

But what happens if one doesn't? And better yet, can it be used as an advantage in a defensive and/or offensive situation?

The quick answers: People generally don't know how to react to unconventional *behavior*. And, of course it can!

For example:

Consider the homeless person on the sidewalk that talks out loud to their non-existent companion.

How do we treat that person?

For the most part (unless we are specifically trying to help the individual) we avoid them and try not to be sucked into their sphere of influence.

Why?

Because they are not acting as we expect them to. They are not acting within our "norms." And as such, it makes us uncomfortable and potentially adds hesitation to our actions; if not fear and/or other emotions (such as sympathy).

> Note: There is a potential overlap with the **Perspective** chapter.

Now consider how this example might be used in a defensive and/or offensive situation. Take tje time to ponder the many potential options and alternatives to this scenario.

The interesting part of the exercise is that it is all based upon *behavior* - nothing else.

What this proves is that *behavior* can be an extremely important element to any social interaction. And as such, can be exploited and potentially used to one's advantage in potentially confrontational situations.

Some abnormal behaviors to contemplate are (usually extreme): anger, timidity, kindness, crazy, aggression, aloofness, and dismissive.

But probably the most important element of using behavior in this way is it must be convincing. Therefore, just like any technique or *drill*, one must practice *behavior* modification.

> Note: There is an overlap with the **Fundamentals** chapter.

> Note: All of this hinges upon human psychology. And, psychology can be used as an **effective strategy**. And as stated above, must be convincing to the opponent(s) in order to succeed.

> Note: There is an overlap with the **Strategy and Theory** section in this chapter.

One extremely important way in which to "sell" *behavior* modification is add detail to the alteration.

As one example:

If one were to choose crazy as their scenario, one might openly drool or vomit on them-self in order to add more credence to the act. Small details such as these can not only help in the deception, but also potentially act as a further deterrent.

Opinion: Vomiting on one's self can also be used as an **effective** deterrent in both conflict and rape scenarios. But like all **behavior** modifying scenarios, one must be aware of any negative consequences of such an act. For instance, in a rape scenario, the attacker may switch to beating (or worse) the defender instead of raping.

The Social Switch

It's one thing to consider *behavior* in the "real world", but what about in the training *environment*?

Can these societal norms effect one's training as well?

Consider the self-defense technique (a.k.a. one-step-sparring) scenario:

Does the attacker attack to hurt? Does the defender counter to hurt? Or, do they "hold back"?

Almost everyone reading this book will have to admit that we don't fully attack or defend with 100% of our abilities.

Why?

Because we don't want to hurt our partner. It's just polite. It wouldn't be nice.

So the question becomes:

Does that effect our ability to perform in the "real world"?

it most certainly does. As stated elsewhere in this book - we will react like we train. And if we train below 100%, we will react below 100%.

> Note: This is stated in the **Reflex vs Thought** section of the **Spontaneity** chapter.

We all have what could be called a *social switch*. A switch that we flip on when we are performing with our partners. This switch makes us act within expected social norms. We don't hit as hard as we can. We don't really try to hurt our partner. etc. And, we are supposed to flip this switch off when it comes to a "real world" scenario.

But, can this be done?

As an example:

In many situations, if one asks their partner to hit them hard when practicing something - really hard or as hard as they can; what will most likely happen?

The partner would hit harder than normal, but not as hard as they possibly could. Probably not nearly hard enough to even injure. Even though they were given the go ahead.

That is the *social switch* in action. And, it shows that it isn't as easy to turn off as one thinks it is.

So how does one solve for this?

One way is to regularly practice turning their *social switch* on and off. Learning when to control the hurt and when to go all out. Not only will this help when it becomes necessary to turn the switch off, it will also help one in learning to dial in the right amount of effort for the situation at hand.

This exercise can add a degree of control that one may not have had before. But the final result is to have control over the *social switch*, not the other way around.

> Note: There is a potential overlap with the **Economy, Efficiency, and Effectiveness** chapter.

> Note/Opinion: Probably the most common way most practitioners try to resolve this issue is to wear some form of body shielding. This gives the attacker piece of mind when really letting loose on their partner.
>
> In general, this is a fairly good method to achieving a similar goal, but the main downside to this form of training is that the attacker never contacts another body, which can potentially lead to imprecise and sloppy technique.
>
> And, also robs the attacker of the distinctive feel of real flesh on flesh.

Strategy and Theory

Literally all maneuvers in the martial arts have purpose, be it explicit or implied. And, ultimately that purpose has an underlying *theory* and/or *strategy* as it's foundation.

Therefore, one of the key tools to analyzing any maneuver or set of maneuvers in any martial art is to first understand what it's motivation (i.e. *strategy / theory*) is.

"Why am I doing this?" "To what end?" "To what effect?"

But, don't be fooled or mollified by a simple answer like:

"to defend myself."

That is not a fundamental *strategy* or *theory*. That is a platitude.

One needs to go further and really get to the root of the issue. The "real deal."

Once this is done, then options, alterations, variations, and expanded avenues of both motion and objectives can then be explored.

In other words, understanding of the why of a what (a.k.a. motion or thought) will lead to exposing the how.

For example:

Take a simple maneuver of defending against a punch. The defender steps into a stance and blocks the punch. Simple enough, but what are the fundamental rationales behind this maneuver?

Questions arise, such as:

"Why did they step into a stance?" "Did they have to?" "Why did they block?" "Did they have to, or is there an alternative?" "What direction did they step and why?" "Where and how did they block the punch and why?" "Was this the start of a bigger strategy or objective?" "Was this maneuver done correctly?"

The interesting thing about all of the answers to the above questions is that it depends. It depends upon the underlying *strategies* and *theories* being applied to the maneuver.

In other words, different *systems* would answer each of the questions differently, based upon the *theories* and *strategies* of that *system*.

That is why one could envision the scenario a hundred different ways by a hundred different *systems* of martial arts.

This elicits the bid question:

"So what?"

But stop to ponder the above statement and its ramifications for a moment. The only way to answer the questions presented is to understand the underlying *principles*, *rules*, *strategies*, and *theories* of the art being applied.

That is an amazing revelation. That simple statement exposes the vastness and ingenuity of the human *mind* at work.

It also lays out the map for understanding the correct details of the maneuver, and understanding how the martial art is applied correctly, from its *perspective*.

> Note: There is an overlap with the **Perspective** and **Principles and Rules** chapters.

So what's the take-away from all of this?

Learning the underlying *strategies* and *theories* help in not only understanding the application and its correctness, but also in how the application can be altered by applying alternative *theories* and *strategies*. These alternatives can be contained within the same *system* or could potentially be borrowed from other *systems*, depending upon the motivations of the practitioner.

Note: There is an overlap with the **Spontaneity** chapter.

Spirituality

From one *perspective*, *spirituality* can be summarized as follows:

One's beliefs around an individual's place within the rest of the universe.

It can attempt to answer large questions such as:

"Why am I here?" "What is my purpose?" "Is there a higher power?" "What comes next?" and other very heady questions.

But it also tries to answer other, almost as heady, but more individualized questions, such as:

"How should I act?" "What is right?" "Should I be good? And, what does that mean?" "How should I interact with my fellow man and nature?"

All these questions and more can directly influence one's interactions, reactions, and actions.

> Note/Opinion: It is acknowledged that philosophy and religion are distinct subjects that also try to answer some of the same questions. But this book is not a debate about *spirituality* vs philosophy vs religion. For the purposes of this chapter, they will all be considered and therefore treated as the same thing.

> Note: There is an overlap with the **Principles and Rules** chapter.

If one pauses only for a moment to contemplate the previous paragraph, it should become relatively clear, very quickly, that *spirituality* can have a dramatic effect on the martial arts and individual practitioners.

And like many other concepts presented in this book, it may be viewed on a *spectrum*. For our purposes that *spectrum* can be called passivity vs violence.

> Note: There is an overlap with the **Spectrum** section of the **Opposites and Reverses** chapter.

This *spectrum* can be described as follows:

On the far end of the passivity side of the *spectrum*, one should believe in total non-violence. Absolutely no harming or injury.

And on the other far end of the violence side of the *spectrum*, one should have no reservations (and potentially no emotions) around killing, maiming, an/or permanently damaging.

The interesting part of the *spectrum* description is that both ends have nothing to do with one's ability and/or skill. Each side could have the exact same skill and ability level. The outcome will all be based upon one's motivations and willingness to control that skill and ability in accordance with their *spiritual* beliefs.

And, that is where martial arts *systems* can be formulated and/or altered.

From a personal *perspective*:

How one perceives their place in the world and how they should interact with other elements of that world (i.e. their *spirituality*) has a dramatic effect on how they will develop and use the skills and knowledge acquired from a martial art.

From a *system perspective*:

Spirituality can be, and often is, the basis for the founding *principles* of specific martial arts.

Combining these two *perspectives* together: One will either develop an art around their own *spirituality*, seek out an art that is compatible with their *spirituality*, or govern their abilities within an art that is not entirely compatible with their belief system. Or finally, not engage in the martial arts at all.

> *Note: There is an overlap with the **Organization, Classification, and Categorization** chapter.*

> *Opinion: When first seeking out an art to train in, one should make an attempt to find an art that is fairly compatible with both their philosophy and their goals.*
>
> *And likewise (**opposite**), an instructor should make an attempt to make sure the art they are teaching is compatible with the potential new student's philosophy.*

> *Note: It is acknowledged that this section is basically a state of **mind** and/or **perspective**, and it could have been grouped within the **mind** section of this chapter or within the **perspective** chapter.*
>
> *But, most people believe that the spirit and **spirituality** is a bigger thing that just a single person's state of **mind**.*
>
> *Therefore **spirituality** was given its own section.*

Morality

Probably the two (2) most important things to understand about *morality* in the martial arts is:

First, *morality* is very subjective (as opposed to objective).

Second, it puts artificial limits on the practitioner.

Combined together, these two (2) attributes of *morality* create a situation where everyone's application of *morality* to their martial art can be slightly different, and therefore create different results and effects upon action and thoughts.

> *Note: It is acknowledged that **morality** and **spirituality** have a large overlap and could have been put into a shared section. But a conscious decision was made to put each in its own section.*

Morality is not, and should not, be confused with a *rule* and/or *principle*. These are objective; meaning they are basically applied to everyone the same, with little to no input from the practitioner's feelings or beliefs.

But *morality*, that's a very different subject. *Morality* has the same outcome as a *rule*, i.e. putting limits on action or thought, but can change dramatically between individuals.

> *Note: There is an overlap with the chapter on **Principles and Rules**.*

Morality is subjective. What does that mean?

It means that your *morality* is based on your personal belief system, opinions and tastes. Because of this, your *morality* is probably not the exact same as someone else's *morality*.

Objective, as expressed above, has exactly the *opposite* definition.

"So, why is this important?"

Because one should never assume that the opponent is working under the same *morality* as they are. This can be a cataclysmic mistake. It can mean the difference between success and failure; and in extreme cases, life and death.

Let's use a weird, yet effective, example:

The movie "The Karate Kid." This movie exposes two (2) very different *moralities*:

The first, Mr. Miyagi's, is relatively passive, plays within social rules and morays, and is slow to be used offensively.

The second, Cobra Ki, is far more aggressive, is willing to break the rules in order to win, and is quick to be used offensively.

This creates a situation where each side must comprehend the opposition in order to apply the appropriate action for any given situations, while staying within their own self-imposed limitations, if any.

The important, yet often overlooked, take-away from this movie is:

Who is right?

We like to think that the passive and kind Mr. Miyagi is the higher *moral* authority:

But, is he right?

It depends upon your *perspective*, *moral* compass, and situational analysis.

Obviously, the Cobra Ki *morality* has a place, given the right social situation. And from their *perspective*, Mr. Miyagi can be taken advantage of and pushed around relatively easy.

From this very raw and naturalistic point of view, passivity could cost one their life.

But again, who is right?

In all reality, they both are.

The movie just frames the situations from a particular societal structure, to influence the viewer to be more sympathetic with the more socially acceptable *morality*.

But in the end, neither is right or wrong.

The important element is that one fully understands that both *moralities* exist and can be applied to effect the actions, and potentially the outcome, of the individuals involved in the situations.

*Note: There is an overlap with the **Perspective** chapter.*

One final thing that should be mentioned about *morality* is it's close association with religion, *spirituality*, and human society.

Often one's actions are tempered by their *spiritual* and/or social beliefs.

For example:

Killing, or not, is almost always tied to either one's *spiritual* beliefs and/or society's willingness to let it occur. And even this limit can be situational and needs to be considered.

War, for example, often absolves the individual of most limits on killing. Also, many civilizations throughout history had no problem with killing or crippling specific individuals.

In the end, though, almost all martial arts are created within specific *moral* structure and each martial artist should fully understand the boundaries of that construct.

Not only how it is applied within its own *moral* boundaries, but how it is appropriately applied to opposing *moral* limitations. And, also what exceptions are acceptable within that *moral* structure and where that martial art allows for and trains for those exceptions, or not.

Part

XVI

Now What?

So, some of the big questions after getting through this book most likely are:

"Is this it?" "Is this everything?" "Is there more?"

The emphatic answer to all of these questions is:

This is just the beginning!

As implied and stated elsewhere throughout this book, the intent of this book is to indoctrinate the reader to essential aspects of thinking on specific subjects. But the martial arts is a huge subject and not all facets of it could ever be covered in such a book as this.

This book is intended to be a guide and launching pad for the reader's own thoughts and discoveries. It's intention is to expand, influence, and lead thought into directions that not many take in the martial arts. Hopefully, it succeeded in that goal.

Also, Its hoped that the reader will use this book as not only a reference but as a motivator into their own exploration into advancing the martial arts.

Maybe a discussion on a specific topic spurred new ideas that have never or rarely been explored and developed.

And further, maybe one of you may use that newly discovered idea into the future development of the martial arts.

But ultimately, the major goal of this book is self-improvement and understanding. With any luck, this book opened eyes and *minds* into *perspectives* of the martial arts that are not often discussed, examined, or explained. And with that, helped each reader, uncover elements of the martial arts that had remained elusive, unknown, or just not thought of before reading this book.

It is hoped that each reader will use this book to better themself and alter their thinking in ways that they may not have expected when originally picking up this book.

And finally, exposed each of you to some of the "knowledge of the grand masters" that may be incorporated into your martial arts and daily life.

Part

XVII

Closing Comments

One criticism that could be leveled at this book may be summed up with the amendment to the phrase presented in the beginning of this book: "He who knows what will be the student. He who knows why will be the instructor. He who knows how will be the master"; combined with the information presented in the chapter *opposites and reverses*.

This criticism would be:

This book only really covers the mental how, not the physical how - i.e. the *opposite* of the mental how.

This was not an oversight, it was intentional.

The dynamics of the physical how are just as important, but are also just as diverse and complex as the mental how; and hence would require, at minimum, another book's worth of information. So, a decision was made to minimize the physical how and attempt to concentrate primarily on the mental how. Also, there are many books on variations of the physical how, but books on the mental how are exceptionally rare.

In closing, it has been the principle intent of this book to expose every reader, to some of the most useful tools and thought *patterns* that the true grand masters of the martial arts have utilized in developing their *systems*. And to, hopefully, guide you all into building upon their success by using and expanding upon these fundamental discoveries and methods.

And maybe, just maybe, help some of you follow in their footsteps of innovation, leadership, and mastery. Have at it and good luck.

www.ingramcontent.com/pod-product-compliance
Lightning Source LLC
Chambersburg PA
CBHW060417100426
42812CB00030B/3216/J